Romantic Deception

THE SIX SIGNS HE'S LYING

Dr. Sally Caldwell

Adams Media Corporation
Holbrook, Massachusetts

Dedication

To the memory of my parents—each with a very
special way of looking at the world.

Published by
Adams Media Corporation
260 Center Street, Holbrook, MA 02343

ISBN: 1-58062-210-0

Printed in the United States of America

J I H G F E D C B

Caldwell, Sally.
Romantic deception: the six signs he's lying / Sally Caldwell.
p.   cm.
ISBN 1-58062-210-0
1. Men—Psychology. 2. Deception. 3. Truthfulness and falsehood.
4. Man-woman relationships. I. Title.
HQ1090.C34   1999
306.7—DC21   99-31862
                          CIP

*This book is available at quantity discounts for bulk purchases.
For information, call 1-800-872-5627.*

Visit our home page at http://www.adamsmedia.com

Table of Contents

Section III: The Six Signs

Section IV: Some Things You Need To Know

Appendix: Survival Guide

Acknowledgments

This book could not have been possible without the women of courage—the women who stepped forward to tell their stories. This book is for, about, and because of them.

By the same token, I could have never seen the project through without the encouragement and support of two very special friends—Eric Groves and Kay Cole. Both were with me when the idea of this book was born, and they remained with me throughout the project. They were always willing to stand back when I needed space and time alone, but were just as quick to return to my side when I needed validation of my efforts.

Finally, I owe so much to my literary agent, Christina Arneson; my editor, Anne Weaver; and my graduate assistant, Allison Moore. Each went the extra mile to make sure the book made the trek from my mind to the printed page.

Preface

I decided to write a book on Romantic Deception because I thought it was an intriguing and compelling topic. I'd known two Romantic Liars in my life—one up close and personal, and the other indirectly at a much safer distance. Both men were rule breakers and renegades, but they were also a lot more. What earned these men the label of Romantic Liar and a special place in the world of problem personalities was their *big-time lying*.

For all practical purposes these men were going through life with fake identities; they were impostors of the first order—men functioning with secret lives and phony resumes and presenting themselves in anything but honest terms. They were lying about everything from their marital status to their military history, and they were also lying to everyone around them, including their intimate partners. And that's what I found so intriguing. The more I thought about the question of deception, particularly how it plays out in intimate relationships, the more intriguing and compelling the topic became.

As soon as I began to look into the literature about deception in intimate relationships, it was obvious to me that very little had ever been written about the topic. There was a lot of information about lying and deception in general, but noticeably absent was anything about lying and deception in the context of intimacy. That's why I decided to do my own research about Romantic Deception and Romantic Liars.

As soon as I went public with the project and started looking for research participants, I realized my topic was more than just intriguing. The reactions I got told me Romantic Deception was very likely a controversial topic. I was immediately hit with questions and criticisms as soon as I placed an ad in the newspaper. The ad made it clear that I was looking for women to interview—women who'd been on the receiving end of Romantic Deception.

Some of the calls were from men who asked if I had any interest in the *male point of view*. They wanted to know if I was going to collect any stories about women who went around duping men. There were also some calls from gays and lesbians who wanted to know if I was going to look at *that* side of deception. Finally there were some obviously angry men who yelled, screamed, and called me names as soon as I answered the phone. As a rule, I didn't say anything to them. I just let them rant and rave. Those were the calls that convinced me the project was touching some nerves, and that it was something *well* worth looking into.

I still get the same questions from friends, colleagues, and total strangers—all seemingly interested in the research I've been doing, but equally curious about my focus. *Isn't it a bit unfair,* they ask, to *look only at one side of the issue? Isn't there a danger in only presenting part of the story?* My answer is the same as it was when I started the project. My aim was to deliver a sound examination of a topic I find truly fascinating, taking an in-depth look and producing something that would have some practical benefit. By definition, that meant I had to narrow the focus.

With a more structured focus, I could look at the questions that really intrigued me. For example:

Do Romantic Liars have predictable traits or characteristics?
Do their lies have a common theme?
Do they have predictable reactions to confrontations?
Do deceptive relationships unfold in a predictable pattern?
Are there certain factors that make a woman vulnerable to
Romantic Deception in the first place?

Some men and women also wondered if this book was going
to be yet another example of male bashing—the sort of book
that has nothing good to say about men. I hope not; that's certainly not what I had in mind. For the record, I'm not into bashing anyone. I also happen to have some truly wonderful men in
my life—men I absolutely adore—who are conversational, witty,
charming, heroic, compassionate, literate, and sexy. I'm especially delighted to add that each one has been a source of
encouragement throughout the project, continually reaffirming
the importance of the project and affording me all the personal
time and space it has required. No, I'm not into male bashing—
just intriguing, compelling topics.

SECTION I

Introduction and Background

Sometimes it's real hard for me to realize that he wasn't the person he said he was. I really cared about the person I thought he was, but that person didn't exist. It's crazy.

Jill, age 27

I remember feeling very stupid. And my intelligence is something that I've always been very proud of. So I was humiliated.

Cindy, age 31

When I interviewed Jill, her mind was still playing tricks on her—shifting back and forth between Michael, the imposter and Michael, the man he really was. The experience nearly drove her crazy as she spent months doing battle with her intuition and suspicion—day after day trying to convince herself that she'd eventually get the answers to Michael's baffling behaviors.

When I interviewed Cindy, the memories of her experience with Kevin were still vivid and painful—particularly, how embarrassed she was when she discovered Kevin was married. Like Jill's experience, Cindy's relationship with Kevin was life-altering—something that would forever change her view of how the world really works.

Both women were also robbed of their sense of trust and felt betrayed. Though the details of their experiences were very different, both stories rested on a common theme—Romantic Deception. Both women had been intimately involved with men who were not who or what they claimed to be.

Jill and Cindy were among the nearly one hundred women who came forward when I went searching for tales about Romantic Liars. Like so many of the other women I interviewed, they were *absolutely insistent* that the word had to get out. As Jill, Cindy, and so many of the other women would eventually say to me, *somebody has to put the word on the street about how the game gets played—somebody's got to let other women know what these guys are up to.*

The introductory material you're about to read is a step in that direction. At a minimum, it will give you a better understanding of what Romantic Deception is all about: what the men are like who play the game and what the consequences are for the women who are targets of deception. Equally important, you'll also learn why there's still so much we don't know when it comes to the world of Romantic Liars and Romantic Deception.

You'll read personal accounts of women who've been on the receiving end of Romantic Deception—case histories that individually tell stories of personal tragedy and accounts that collectively serve to warn us about the dangers of Romantic Deception. You'll also be introduced to the issue of vulnerability in a way that might cause you to think twice—particularly if you've been operating on the assumption that Romantic Deception is something that happens only to other women.

So You Think He Might Be Lying

OK. So you're involved in a relationship—one that started out like it had a lot of promise. As a matter of fact, all the right chemistry was there from the very start, or so it seemed. The relationship took off like a rocket, and before you knew what happened, you were thinking *this might be the one. Nearly perfect*, or so you thought.

But now something is wrong. As a matter of fact, something is dreadfully wrong. You can't put your finger on it, but something's not right. It's a thought that races through your mind; it's an eerie feeling in the pit of your stomach. Something is wrong, but you don't know what it is. Welcome to the world of Romantic Deception.

Let's say you're a little further along in the relationship. If so, the strain is probably starting to take its toll. You're starting to get a little worn down emotionally. Chances are you're waging a one-woman battle to retain your own sanity; the contradictions and inconsistencies are more than you can take. You may even be obsessing about what's going on with the relationship, but you don't have the courage to openly question your partner.

The feelings and sensations I just described may be your first clue that you're involved with a Romantic Liar—a man who's been lying about who and what he is. The web of deceit no doubt started weeks or months ago, but now you're getting in deeper. Unfortunately, you probably don't have a clue about what's really going on. It's possible you're starting to act a little crazy. Welcome to Romantic Deception writ large.

This book is about Romantic Deception and Romantic Liars—men who create false identities for your consumption. It's about Romantic Deception from the first stage, when you're getting hooked on your partner, to the fourth stage, when you decide to leave the relationship (even though you find that hard to do or you make several unsuccessful attempts). It's about how the game of Romantic Deception is played and why you and thousands of other women just like you are highly vulnerable. This book is also about the men who turn out to be Romantic Liars—how they go about their craft of Romantic Deception and why they get away with it.

If you've read this far, you're curiosity is piqued. That's good. At a minimum, I'd guess you're trying to figure out an answer to a question that's been nagging at you. I can't promise this book will give you *all* the answers you're looking for, but it will point you in the right direction. It will also give you information about clues to deceit—valuable information that can save you a lot of heartache down the road.

It may be that you're already so far into a deceptive relationship that you're now struggling to find a way out. That's another good sign. Hopefully this book will help you break free. Deceptive relationships are highly destructive on any number of fronts. They're toxic and fraught with danger. No matter where you are in the Deception Dynamic, you've got some tough work to do.

If there's the slightest hint in your mind that you've gotten involved with someone who's lying to you, it's time to get a grip. At the very least, you owe it to yourself to look beneath the surface. Deceptive relationships have a way of appearing very different from what they actually are. Indeed, most deceptive relationships start out with an extraordinary amount of mutual attraction between the people involved, and they're usually laced with an abundance of romance. They're also punctuated with a high degree of passion, and fueled with what looks like total commitment from your partner.

In the midst of all that it's tough to step back and take a serious look at what may be going on beneath the surface of your relationship. Like I said, deceptive relationships are usually very seductive. But something has caused you to read this far, so you owe it to yourself to keep going. Your partner may turn out to be as genuine as the day is long, and he may be exactly who and what he says he is. If that's the case, so much the better. On the other hand, what if he's not? What if he's actually a Romantic Liar?

If you've just met someone, ask yourself . . .

1. Does the relationship strike you as almost too good to be true?
2. Does he know far more about you than you know about him?
3. Does he want to know everything about your past relationships?
4. Is he often in situations where you can't reach him?
5. Are you still waiting for him to give you a home telephone number?
6. Do you spend almost all of your free time with him?
7. Do you spend most of your time together by yourselves?
8. Has he been able to keep you away from his home or place of work?
9. Are you still waiting to meet his family or friends?

If you've been involved with this man for a while, ask yourself . . .

1. If you question him, does he *turn the tables on you* and doubt your trust in him?
2. Is he critical of you?
3. Is he critical of your friends and family or has he limited your contact with them?
4. Does he call you several times a day to see what you're doing?
5. Is he calling frequently to ask what your plans are or where you might be going?

6. Has he been critical of your job or has he asked you to quit your job?
7. Have you been the object of physical or verbal abuse?
8. Does he ever go into a rage at the slightest provocation or for no apparent reason?
9. Are you always *walking on eggshells* to prevent any further abuse?
10. Does he abuse drugs or alcohol?
11. Does he show signs of unwarranted jealousy?

So, how many questions did you answer with a *yes*? Unfortunately there's no magic score on that informal quiz, just as there aren't any easy ways to determine right off the bat if you're being Romantically Deceived. No wonder. Romantic Deception, by its very nature, is cloaked in secrecy, manipulation, and illusion.

A Romantic Liar isn't the man who tells a *little white lie* now and then to keep your spirits up or fails to tell you the *whole truth* because he wants to *spare your feelings*. By the same token, a Romantic Liar isn't the man who adds an *embellishment here or there* just to make a good impression on you when you first meet. Omissions and enhancements like that technically constitute lying, but they don't qualify as Romantic Deception. As you'll soon learn, Romantic Deception is far more.

Masters in the art of Romantic Deception get away with the game because they are just that—*masters*. They know what to do and how to do it. When a Romantic Liar is operating in top form, you probably won't have a clue about what's going on. Some Romantic Liars specialize in concealing the fact that they're married, while others have a flair for posing as doctors or lawyers when they're not. Some Romantic Liars like to present themselves as decorated war heroes; others go a step further by impersonating intelligence agents for the federal government. As a rule, a Romantic Liar is limited only by his imagination and the immediate circumstances. The list of lies a Romantic Liar might tell you is a long one.

Because he's capable of lying about anything and everything imaginable, there's no limit to the ways a Romantic Liar can harm you. You can lose substantial amounts of money to a Romantic Liar, and you might lose your job or career because of him. You might avoid the financial loss but suffer the emotional or physical consequences. Even if you're a self-assured, intelligent, and resourceful woman, you'll probably end up with a shaken self-image when you realize you were duped. Therapists' offices are full of women who've been the targets of Romantic Deception. Maybe you're one of them. If you are, you would do well to always remember: Romantic Deception is something that happens to thousands of women every day. You're not alone.

If you discover you're a target of deception, but you find out early enough to make a swift exit, consider yourself lucky. More than likely, though, the game's been going on long enough that now you find yourself emotionally hooked on your partner. If that's the case, you'll probably find yourself having to deal with a hefty amount of emotional damage. The aftermath of Romantic Deception is a fairly predictable emotional nightmare.

You'll probably go through a gut-wrenching experience when you try to untangle your feelings and understand how it happened. More than likely your first question will be *why didn't I know what was going on?* At some point you'll be hit with a profound sense of loss over a relationship you thought was meaningful. The sense of loss will grow even more confusing when you begin to recognize that *who* or *what* you were in love with didn't really exist in the first place.

The list goes on. Self-doubt, sleepless nights, deep depressions. Weight loss, weight gain, anger, and resentment. Substance abuse or casual sex as temporary escapes. Embarrassed attempts to regain contact with friends you dropped along the way. The range of emotions is wide, but you'll almost certainly return to your original question—*Why didn't I know?*

Of course, not every man who tries his hand at Romantic Deception gets away with it. Every day thousands of married men try to pass themselves off as being single, and even more try to embellish who they are. Even so, many of these would-be Romantic Liars fail. These men may have the bravado to attempt their hand at Romantic Deception, but they lack the necessary skills to really pull it off.

There are other men, however, who fall into a very different category. These are men who are skilled at the game of deception beyond your wildest imagination. They're *masters in the art of deception,* so much so that the charade can go on for months or years. Consider the following cases:

Case #1

Taylor Worthen, M.D., Parkhurst Hospital. Pathology. Across the bottom of his hospital badge was his picture and the illegible signature you'd expect out of a physician. It was all right there. But it was Taylor's British accent that first caught Allison's attention.

Allison knew right away that Taylor wasn't an everyday, run-of-the-mill pickup artist. He wasn't the jerk who gets your telephone number, says he'll call, and never does. No, Taylor Worthen, M.D., was very different. More than anything else, he was a gentleman. Taylor, the transplanted Englishman, remained a gentleman for the nearly six months of his relationship with Allison. They had dinner at the nicest places as he squired her around in his new Mercedes. Despite his busy schedule as a physician trying to get established in this country, Taylor was extremely attentive.

On occasion they went out to his new house in the upscale country club area, but most of the time they stayed at Allison's apartment closer to the hospital. It was a comfortable relationship. If Allison ever had a problem or needed to get in touch with Taylor, all she had to do was call his answering service. Allison thought everything was just fine. Then she learned the truth from the local police.

Taylor Worthen, M.D., wasn't a doctor, and he wasn't from England (even though he could rise from a dead sleep speaking in a British accent). No, Taylor Worthen was actually from Iowa, and he was working as the chauffeur for the man who owned the lovely home and luxury automobile. Taylor also had a pretty lengthy arrest record.

Case #2

Carole, thirty years old and recently divorced, was skeptical at first. The relationship seemed to be just a little too wonderful from the start. Bill was an attorney with a promising career in a corporate environment. Without the pressures to build a client base, Bill always had time for Carole.

Despite Carole's skepticism, the romance took off like a rocket. Bill was calling two and three times a day, showing up with flowers, regularly scheduling romantic dinners, and constantly showering her with affection.

A few weeks into their relationship, though, Bill and Carole had to put the torrid romance on temporary hold; Bill had to make a business trip to California. He went by Carole's office before he left, just to say good-bye and to give her a long-stemmed rose. He called her every day while he was away, each time telling her how anxious he was to get back. After Bill returned, the starry-eyed couple took up where they had left off. They saw each other almost every night. Bill was always around. The romance continued that way for about eight months.

Then, quite by accident, Carole learned the truth. Bill's business trip was really his honeymoon. That's right. Bill married another woman within a few weeks of meeting Carole. He just didn't bother to let Carole know about it.

Case #3

Even though they had been seeing each other on an exclusive basis for more than a year and were virtually living together at Sharon's apartment, Dan still kept his own place (saying he was still not quite ready for a commitment and not totally ready to give up his personal space). Everything seemed to be going all right, but a voice inside told Sharon that something was wrong. Even though she had her suspicions, Sharon tried to put the nagging thought out of her mind. Finally her curiosity and churning stomach got the best of her. Sharon decided to do some snooping. That's when she uncovered Dan's telephone records.

A quick look at the phone bills convinced her that Dan was seeing someone else. There were just too many calls to the same number in a nearby suburb. With a little help from a friend, Sharon was able to learn that her suspicions had some basis in fact; someone named Amy was the other woman in Dan's life.

Sharon eventually mustered the courage to call Amy, but the reception was anything but positive. Amy figured Sharon was just a jealous ex-girlfriend from Dan's past, and she made it clear to Sharon that she didn't want to be bothered. Persuaded that Amy hadn't gotten the message, Sharon was determined to make her point. To do that, Sharon faxed the telephone logs to Amy—just to prove that she had access to Dan's personal records. That's what turned the tide in this saga that includes yet one more woman.

The faxed phone records got Amy's attention, at least to the point where she decided to give them a closer look. What Amy discovered was a string of telephone calls to still another number in another suburb—one that Sharon had obviously overlooked in her earlier sleuthing. Amy faxed the materials back to Sharon with the newly discovered number circled for emphasis. Now the two women bonded; they started on their mission together.

Amy and Sharon finally located Laurel (Woman #3) and decided to confront her at her home. The encounter was bizarre, and Laurel was shocked and confused, to say the least. Two women Laurel had never seen in her life had pulled in behind her as she was getting out of her car in front of her home. Sharon and Amy had enough evidence with them to quickly convince Laurel she was the third woman in the mess. The scene got a little out of control at first, but that was only because the trio was still in the front yard when Laurel started crying uncontrollably.

When the calm finally settled in, the three women compared notes and swapped stories. Dan was obviously on the top of the chart as far as sexual stamina; he'd managed to see each of them three or four times a week. He'd also managed to convince each woman that she was the only woman in his life.

The three women decided to confront Dan when he returned from a business trip to Tulsa. Sharon's apartment was the staging area (Dan was scheduled to arrive there when he got into town). Sharon was poised for the greeting; Amy was hiding in the bathroom; and Laurel was tucked away in the loft area above the living room. The video camera was on top of the refrigerator and aimed to record the festivities.

Dan had just crossed the threshold when he started telling Sharon how glad he was to be home and how much he missed her. That was Amy's cue. She popped out of the bathroom and asked, *What about me?* Before he could answer, Laurel popped her head over the loft railing and asked the same question.

Dan's response to this confrontation? A simple but rather emphatic *You mean I just drove all the way from Tulsa for this shit?*

Those are just a few of the cases that surfaced when I started my search for women who'd experienced Romantic Deception. Extreme, you ask? Not really. Not any more so than any of the other cases I heard about in my research.

Other cases include the stories of women who became involved in long-distance relationships only to find out they were being used as a *mistress* and women who discovered they had been duped out of money. In some cases it was a man claiming to have a string of credentials that turned out to be totally bogus. In others, it was a man who was spinning all sorts of tales of personal tragedy in an apparent aim to win the sympathies of an unsuspecting target. This book is based on the personal hell that women went through when they found out they'd been the targets of deception. Sure, some cases might strike you as more dramatic than others, but all the cases were jolting to the one on the receiving end of the deceit.

Each case has its own peculiar twist and turn, yet there were remarkable similarities across the stories—how the relationship got started, what the men lied about, the strategies they used in spinning their lies, and how they reacted when they were eventually confronted. There were also remarkable similarities in how the women felt when they realized they'd been deceived. Most of the women were well on their way to recovery when I interviewed them, but others were still trying to make sense of it all.

The women were from all walks of life, and there were significant differences in their backgrounds. I heard from women who'd grown up in modest circumstances; I heard from others who'd enjoyed far more. Some of the victims were highly educated and working in lucrative careers; others were struggling. There was only one common denominator: All of the women had been victims of Romantic Deception.

Whenever I've included a woman's personal story, I've tried to remain true to her experience, yet sensitive to her need for anonymity. I've altered names, places, and occupations—all in an effort to respect my subjects' privacy. That's the least I can do. It takes great courage for some women to step forward and tell their personal tales of deceit. Indeed, a sense of personal embarrassment seems to go hand in hand with being the target of Romantic Deception.

Women who have been targets of Romantic Deception also know what it's like to live in a society culturally programmed to blame the victim, and their words can be powerful.

You know, I've tried to figure out how this happened to me. This deal totally devastated me, so I tried to figure it out. I'm still trying to figure it out. I read all these relationship books and stuff and I'm ready to scream. I'm up to here with people saying there was something wrong with me. If I hear one more word of that psychological crap, I'm going to go nuts. Nobody ever says a word about the bastard that made my life miserable. Nobody ever says anything about what a sleaze he was. Nobody ever says anything except it was my fault to begin with.

Elizabeth, age 36

After I found out what he was all about, I was totally embarrassed 'cause I felt so stupid. I usually don't talk to people about it 'cause they wouldn't understand. These guys are real smooth—that's what people don't understand. You meet a guy and he tells you this and that and he makes it sound true. And that's what people don't understand. They think you got into the mess because you were just too blind to see. I'm telling you—people who think that's the way it is are the ones who don't get it.

Anna, age 24

If the words you just read echo your feelings, take heart. On any given day there are thousands of women just like you—women still struggling to make sense of a deceptive relationship. Like you, these women know very well how the game of Romantic Deception is played. Like you, they know what it's like to try to give voice to their experience. With all the blame that's put on victims in our society, it's little wonder that victims of deceptive relationships choose to take their feelings underground. If you're in that category—someone who's taken her experience of Romantic Deception underground—read on. This book might help you come to grips with the experience. I can't promise you it will be easy. In fact, you've got some very tough work ahead of you. But you can do it—that's the important message—so let's get started.

Romantic Deception:
Definitions and Dimensions

If you want to understand Romantic Deception, it's best to start with a *technical* definition—one that tells you what Romantic Deception *is* and what it *isn't*. Here's the definition that I like to use:

> Romantic Deception is the unrestrained misrepresentation of significant facts in the context of an intimate relationship.

Since Romantic Deception involves a special sort of lying in special circumstances, it pays to take a closer look.

Romantic Deception Involves Unrestrained Behavior

Make no mistake about it. Romantic Liars are *unrestrained* in their deception. They're capable of lying about anything and everything under the sun. When a Romantic Liar starts lying, nothing stands in his way, and no topic is sacred. What's more, most Romantic Liars have trouble stopping with just one lie. To understand what *unrestrained lying* is all about, consider the case of Brenda, a systems analyst in her early forties.

Brenda had been going with Ted for about four months, and she had no reason to think anything was wrong with the relationship. In fact, Brenda thought it was solid enough to invite Ted to meet her family during the holidays. It was actually Rick, Brenda's older brother, who became suspicious—so much so that he decided to do a little digging into Ted's background.

Brenda was upset when Rick told her what he'd done, but she got over it when he told her what he'd discovered. Ted had actually left the community college in mid-semester of his first year, even though he claimed to be a graduate of Arizona State. Besides that, Ted had somehow forgotten to mention one of his two ex-wives, and the heroic military record he bragged about was totally fabricated.

When you consider the important elements in that story—how Ted embellished some parts of his identity while remaining totally silent about others—you sense what unrestrained lying really means. For Ted, no lie was too big, no topic was too sacred, no lie was one too many.

Romantic Deception Is about Misrepresentation

Romantic Liars don't just openly lie or speak falsehoods. Truly skilled Romantic Liars use all sorts of techniques to paint a false picture. That's why I use the term *misrepresentation* to describe what's at the heart of Romantic Deception. Romantic Liars tell straight-out lies, to be sure, but they also engage in overstatement and understatement. Sometimes Romantic Liars lie through their silence, and sometimes they deceive with the help of friends.

If you think the only lies that count are the ones coming out of someone's mouth, you're in for a rude awakening when it comes to a Romantic Liar. Some actually say very little, but *misrepresent* a lot. Indeed, most Romantic Liars are quite content to let you draw your own conclusions. Among the various forms of misrepresentation available to a Romantic Liar are the following:

- *Falsification*—deliberate statements of false information. For example, he claims he was the captain of the varsity football squad, but he's never seen the inside of a college classroom, let alone the team's locker room.

- *Concealment*—withholding important information in an effort to promote or sustain a false impression. For example, he tells you he's been an insurance adjuster for fourteen years, but he fails to mention he hasn't worked a day since he was laid off eight months ago.

- *Diversion*—redirection of a conversation, particularly when it involves direct questions. For example, you ask straightforward questions about his work or recent divorce, and he changes the subject or says he wants to talk about you.

- *Exaggeration*—embellishment and inflation of story elements to enhance a personal position or create a false impression. For example, he tells you he's a senior manager for an electronics manufacturer, but he's actually a clerk in the shipping department.

- *Understatement*—minimizing or downplaying significant events in his personal history. For example, he tells you he went through a *messy* divorce, but he doesn't say anything about the restraining orders his ex-wife took out on him.

Romantic Deception Involves Significant Facts

Romantic Deception involves *facts*—not emotions and feelings or predictions about the future. For example, Romantic Deception *isn't* about a man telling you he's going to love you forever or saying he can't imagine a life without you. All of us have heard things like that at one time or another (particularly in the throes of passion), but that doesn't qualify as Romantic Deception.

On the other hand, it *is* a matter of deception when your partner starts making false statements of *fact*. When he does that, he's beyond the world of emotions, feelings, or predictions about the future and he's into the world of Romantic Deception. Here's what Romantic Liars commonly lie about:

- *Marital Status*—lies about whether he's married, how many times he's been married, and what happened to his ex-wife (or wives), etc.
- *Family Relationships*—lies about the number of children he has, which family members are still living, and where they live, etc.
- *Personal History*—lies about where he grew up, where he went to school, whether or not he served in the military, etc.
- *Present Circumstances and Lifestyle*—lies about where he actually lives and who he's living with, where he works or what he does for a living, etc.

Romantic Deception Is Something that Plays Out in Intimate Relationships

All of us are accustomed to being on the receiving end of a lie now and then—lies from coworkers, acquaintances, politicians, and any number of other people. As a result, most of us have probably learned to tolerate some degree of lying. As a rule, though, the closer we are to the source of the lie, the more harmful the effect tends to be.

It's one thing if we're lied to by a politician, but it's quite another when it's our intimate partner. And that's what puts Romantic Deception in a category of its own. Romantic Deception is a breach of trust, and it negates the very essence of intimacy. Here's why:

- *Intimacy is based upon self-disclosure*, but self-disclosure is the last thing on the mind of a Romantic Liar. Your partner may encourage you to share your deepest feelings—everything from your fears to your hopes and dreams—and, in the interest of building an intimate relationship, you're likely to go along the road of self-disclosure, operating on the assumption that it's a two-way street. But that has nothing to do with whether or not your partner is going to be honest in his self-disclosures to you.

- *Intimacy is based upon a presumption of honesty,* but honesty is not part of a Romantic Liar's value system. It's hard to imagine that anyone would enter into an intimate relationship with any thought other than being honest, but that's exactly what goes on in a case of Romantic Deception. You may presume that your partner is being honest with you (after all, you reason, it's an intimate relationship, right?), but that's merely a presumption on your part.

- *Intimacy is based upon trust,* but any sense of trust you have in a relationship with a Romantic Liar is hollow. In an intimate relationship, the element of trust extends to physical and emotional well-being and you feel a sense of safety when you're with your partner. The more you trust someone, the more you're willing to surrender yourself. In doing so, the more vulnerable you become.

Because Romantic Deception involves an absence of every important element in an intimate relationship, its no wonder that a relationship with a Romantic Liar can turn out to be an emotional nightmare. As I mentioned before, it is common for victims of Romantic Deception to look back on the experience as a life-altering event—one that brought to the surface the widest range of emotions and one that forever colors how they will look at the world.

All of what you've been reading tells you what Romantic Deception is about in technical terms, but it hardly touches on what it's like to be in a deceptive relationship. Regardless of where you might be in a relationship with a Romantic Liar, here are some things you need to know about deceptive relationships in general.

Deceptive Relationships Are Toxic

When I say a deceptive relationship is toxic, I mean it can leak into every area of your life. There are two reasons behind that. First, Romantic Liars generally turn out to be men who have controlling personalities—they're the sort of men who want to run every aspect of your life. I talked to some women who actually described their Romantic Liars as anything but controlling, but the women in that category numbered less than a handful. By far the majority of women eventually came to view their partners as extremely controlling in any number of ways.

Second, being locked in a deceptive relationship can make you crazy. Like any sort of deception, successful misrepresentation by a Romantic Liar normally requires some sabotage of your perceptual abilities. In other words, he'll have to make you think what isn't true is true and what is true isn't. In a game like that, it's little wonder that so many targets of Romantic Deception eventually get to the point that they think their losing they're grip on reality.

Add them together—the controlling aspects and the sabotaging behavior—and you have the right mix for a truly toxic relationship. Here are just a few examples of how bad a relationship with a Romantic Liar can get:

- *Disturbance of Family and Social Network:* It's common for a victim of deception to find her contact with family, friends, and acquaintances is more and more limited as the relationship goes on. Take the case of Julie. When she discovered Ned was actually married, her world crumbled in around her and she sank into a deep depression. When she finally found the strength to reach out for help, she discovered her friendship network had virtually disappeared. Partly in an effort to spend time with Ned, but partly because Ned was always so critical of her friends, Julie had systematically withdrawn from her familiar social circle. When the time came that she really needed them, Julie's friends were few and far between.

- *Disruption of Work or Career:* Your job or career is but one more of your links to the outside world, so it shouldn't surprise you that a Romantic Liar may take steps to undermine that area of your life, as well. Sandy, for example, was getting further and further behind in her work—partly because Jason, her new boyfriend, was calling all the time and interrupting her at work just to ask her what she was doing. He was also asking her to meet him for long lunches on a regular basis. All that eventually caught up with her; Sandy lost her job. Jason told Sandy not to worry; he'd take care of her until she found another job. At least, that's what he said. But there was just one problem. Jason didn't have a job either. He was actually living off another girlfriend.

- *Reorientation of Activities and Future Plans:* Give a Romantic Liar half a chance and he'll tell you how to spend your every waking moment. Deloris, for example, had been a regular in an art class for more than two years, but that was before she met Randy. At first Randy was able to persuade her to miss her class just to spend time with him. Later on, though, Randy became more insistent that she put aside her art classes altogether. When he started criticizing her abilities and telling her it was downright silly for her to think that she'd ever be an artist, Deloris gave in and gave up.

Deceptive Relationships Can Be Addictive

Deceptive relationships generally have a highly addictive quality. Why wouldn't they? After all, a deceptive relationship is one a Romantic Liar crafted with you in mind. It rests on his ability to present just the right image—an image that you'll find hard to resist. But the lies are not the source of the addiction; the dynamics of the relationship give rise to the addictive quality.

Because they are characteristically controlling and even abusive, Romantic Liars frequently vent their anger on their partners. But like many other men in the same category, Romantic Liars are quick to seek forgiveness. They are angry or abusive one minute and begging to be taken back the next. When this type of pattern creeps into the interaction between two people, the relationship is ripe for addiction to take hold. The stage is set for the destructive game of reward and punishment. There's something incredibly seductive about the power that goes along with a pattern of intermittent rewards; that's why addictions are so tough to break. Here are some typical signs of an addictive relationship—all of which are amazingly characteristic of deceptive relationships, as well:

- You know the relationship is bad for you for all sorts of reasons, but you won't take the necessary steps to leave. For every reason to leave, you find a reason to stay.
- Even though you're aware of the bad things about the relationship, you find a way to minimize or downplay them. You tell yourself that things will get better. You may start blaming yourself for all the problems—telling yourself that things will improve if you change *your* behavior.
- If you eventually take steps to leave your partner, you find it is difficult to stay away from him. You're very likely to repeatedly re-establish the relationship. The addictive power of the relationship continues to pull you back toward your partner.
- With all your energies focused on your partner and the relationship, you find it impossible to imagine yourself in different circumstances. Even though the relationship you're in is destructive or even dangerous, you see it as something that is exciting. Other partners, if you even thought about them, would strike you as boring.

Deceptive Relationships Are Destructive and Dangerous

Deceptive relationships are destructive and potentially dangerous on several levels. Everything you have, from your material possessions to your emotional well-being, can be damaged or destroyed. When you're mixed up with a Romantic Liar, the list of areas where you're vulnerable is long. For example:

- *Financial Resources and Property:* Though not as common as a lot of people think, some Romantic Liars eventually do make a run on a victim's financial resources. A Romantic Liar might ask you for a friendly loan and then never bother to repay you. He might also make use of your credit cards without your knowledge. Melinda, for example, discovered the money she loaned Charles actually went to pay for his other girlfriend's breast implants. Melody, on the other hand, found out her credit card financed the plane ticket Al used when he left town in the middle of the night. Since most deceptive relationships are likely to turn abusive, your personal property is also at risk when you're dealing with a Romantic Liar. Beware of the potential dangers when you make the decision to confront or leave a Romantic Liar. Sarah, for example, found her home totally ransacked when she came home from work one day. She could never prove what happened, but the fact that she had confronted Derrick the night before convinced her he was the likely suspect.

- *Emotional Health:* A relationship with a Romantic Liar usually turns into an emotional train wreck. You'll more than likely experience every negative emotion you can think of—everything from anger to depression to shame and embarrassment. What's worse, the emotional strain will be there throughout much of the relationship. The unpredictability of your partner's behavior will throw you off guard fairly early in the relationship. From that point forward, you'll be in a downward spiral.

- *Physical Health:* The long-term effects of the emotional strain will ultimately affect your physical health. Depression is a common reaction to involvement with a Romantic Liar, and predictably, many victims of Romantic Deception experience significant changes in dietary habits.

Significant weight loss or weight gain is common. Throw in the alterations in normal sleep patterns that so frequently accompany depression and you have a situation tailor-made for physical illness. Beyond all of that there's always the risk of contracting a sexually transmitted disease. Protected sex is the safest policy with any partner, let alone a Romantic Liar. Finally victims of Romantic Deception routinely find themselves on the receiving end of physical abuse. That alone warrants treating a relationship with a Romantic Liar as a dangerous activity.

Some Rules of Thumb

As you'll eventually learn, each case of Romantic Deception is unique, and there's no predicting how any given relationship with a Romantic Liar will unfold. At the same time, though, there are certain things you can almost count on when you get involved with a Romantic Liar—so much so that there are a few *rules of thumb* you should pay attention to. For example:

- *Rule #1: The Longer You're in a Deceptive Relationship, the Worse It is Likely to Get.* Deceptive relationships don't improve; they just get worse. Any hope you have that a Romantic Liar will change is just wishful thinking. Two things tend to escalate over time in deceptive relationships—the amount of lying that takes place, and the amount of control your partner will try to exert over you. The increase in the number of lies will only make you crazier and crazier, often to the point that you think you're losing your mind. Your partner's desire to control you can ultimately lead to physical violence. Your sanity and personal safety are too important to risk just because you think a bad situation will improve over time.
- *Rule #2: If You Sense that Your Intuition Is Talking to You, Listen to It.* If your inner voice starts to make noises, listen to it. If your stomach starts to knot up, sense it. Never dismiss your intuitive powers when it comes to personal

relationships, even though you might find a hundred reasons to do so. If you're someone who takes pride in being rational or logical or analytical, that's fine. Just don't let that rule out making use of your other powers. When you understand what intuition is all about (see Section III), you'll know why it's such a powerful ally.

- *Rule #3: If Your Friends Starting Talking to You about the Relationship, Listen.* If you're blessed to have a circle of friends who are willing to tell you the truth as they see it, count your blessings. Friends like that are valuable in any number of situations. If you're entangled in a deceptive relationship, your friends may be able to recognize it long before you do. If they start dropping hints or, better yet, if they come right out and tell you they think something's amiss, listen to them. Your friend's judgments may be far more objective than yours, particularly if you're still caught up in the early stages of a deceptive relationship and the passion is at an all-time high.

- *Rule #4: The Greater the Number of Lies, the More Disturbed He Is Apt to Be.* It's one thing if your partner tells you that he has two children from a previous marriage when he actually has three, or he represents he has an M.B.A. when he's actually a grade-school dropout. Both are gross misrepresentations, to be sure, and both signal his willingness to deceive you. Your partner is in another category altogether, though, if his lies and misrepresentations reach the point that he is a total impostor, presenting a false picture of everything about his past right up to his present-day circumstances. It's safe to say that most Romantic Liars are psychologically or emotionally troubled to some extent and they have a need to present an enhanced public image. The question, of course, is how far he will go to present the false image. At the furthermost end of the spectrum are the more dramatic cases—the Romantic Liars who fabricate a totally false image. The examples are legion: Men who claim to have been war heroes, men who

pose as doctors or attorneys, men who claim to be working as agents for the federal government. When it gets to
that level of deception, it's safe to say that the men are
severely disturbed.

But What Do We Really Know?

A definition of Romantic Deception gets us on the road to
understanding what the phenomenon is all about, but there are
still a lot of unanswered questions. For example, *What are the
characteristics of a Romantic Liar? What about the characteristics of
deceptive relationships?* To answer those questions, let's first look
at what we know about deception in general. Then we'll turn to
the specific case of Romantic Deception.

The Scorecard on Deception Research

When it comes to the mysterious world of deceit, misrepresentation, liars, and such, the truth is a little unsettling. There's
still a lot that we just don't know. Deception, as a topic of
inquiry, has caught the attention of a lot of researchers, but
there's so much that still remains a mystery. Unfortunately, I suspect that's the way it's going to be for quite a while.

A lot of the problem stems from the fact that most deception
research is conducted in laboratory or experimental situations—
environments far removed from real life and even more removed
from the reality of intimate relationships. We always have to ask
the question of whether or not the findings would apply to
deception in real-life situations.

Beyond that, the findings and discoveries from the laboratory and experimental situations are often inconclusive, at best.
For example, some deception detection studies have found that
a group of college students perform no better or worse than

members of the law enforcement community when it comes to identifying which of two or more research participants is lying in an experimental situation. It's also safe to say that most deception research is focused on deception detection. When it comes to the question of what *motivates* a liar to lie in the first place, we're still very much in the dark.

If we were ever to fully investigate *real-life* deception, as opposed to deception in laboratory settings, we would eventually have to delve into the world of the person telling the lies. And that may pose the biggest problem of all. We really know very little about deception detection to begin with, but we know even less about liars. Two monumental problems stand in our way.

First, significant liars (i.e., people who make it a practice to lie on a regular basis) are rarely available for study. In a word or two, liars are *reluctant subjects*. Don't count on a Romantic Liar or any other big-time liar to march into a counselor's office because his lying has become a problem. The fact that he lies on a regular basis might be a problem for his girlfriend or any number of other people, but it isn't a problem for him. In fact, for someone like a Romantic Liar, the lying may be the very thing that allows him to cope with a scarred identity. The lying may be the one thing that lets him get through the day with his self-image intact.

Second, there's a serious question as to whether or not you could believe anything a liar said in the first place. If someone is the sort who lies on a frequent basis in any number of circumstances, there's actually little reason to presume he would stop his lying in the interest of scientific inquiry. Even if you had the luxury of interviewing a serious liar—say in a clinical setting, for example—it would be difficult to put much faith in what he told you about anything.

The Characteristics of Romantic Liars

I was able to get *some idea* of what Romantic Liars are like because I collected case histories from their victims, but even so, the picture of Romantic Liars is still far from complete. Most of the women I interviewed were able to conclude with absolute certainty that their partner had lied about some things, but they also had the haunting feeling that much about their partner was still a mystery. For example, here's what Jenny said when I asked her to discuss all the lies Fred told her.

> *You know what? I still don't know how much of it was a lie. I know he lied when he told me he was divorced. I know that was a lie 'cause I got a call from his wife. I also know he lied about his job. Now that I think back on it, I'm pretty sure he was lying about where he went to school, too, but I really don't know. Same thing about where he grew up and all—I think he probably invented a lot of that, but I really don't know.*

And that's what happens in so many cases of Romantic Deception. The relationship ends, and the victim is left with the disturbing thought that she never knew her partner at all.

Given a situation like that, it stands to reason that it would be difficult to build an accurate profile of Romantic Liars. At best, all we have are glimpses and hints of what they're really like; it's not much to go on. Nonetheless, there are a few things you *should* and *shouldn't* expect when it comes to a Romantic Liar:

- Don't expect a Romantic Liar to fit into any certain age group. He can be a young man in his twenties or a senior citizen in his sixties. Most of the men I heard about in my interviews were in their thirties and forties, but I have to tell you that the ones in their mid- to late-twenties were also quite numerous. By far the majority of Romantic Liars I learned about were married men who were cheating on their wives, but many are single or divorced. The notion that most Romantic Liars are middle-aged, married men trying to find a way to deal with a woefully unhappy marriage is simply a myth; there's also a whole bunch of single men running around with phony identities.

- Romantic Liars aren't always the high rollers you read about in the newspaper or see portrayed in made-for-television movies. They have blue-collar occupations as often as they have white-collar occupations, and they're more apt to be employed than unemployed. Whatever their occupation, however, it's common for them to be in some sort of job or career that gives them flexibility in their daily schedules.

- As much as anything, most Romantic Liars are inclined to lie about their educational background. They routinely make false claims about colleges and universities they supposedly attended, and they have a habit of bestowing degrees upon themselves that are anything but legitimate. In the interviews I heard about a far greater number of men with Ph.D. degrees than you could expect in the general population, and I heard about more M.B.A.s than I could count. The fact that Romantic Liars have a habit of lying about their educational background can actually work in your favor. As you'll learn in Section IV, formal education credentials are actually fairly easy to verify.

- It's also very common for a Romantic Liar to have some rather unusual living arrangements when you first meet him. For example, he may tell you he's sharing a home with another man or he's just moved into a small apartment because he's *in the middle of some sort of transition* (whatever that means). Romantic Liars are forever planning on moving into new surroundings—a larger apartment or bigger house. If you're hanging out with a Romantic Liar who's cheating on his wife, don't be surprised if he takes you to look at a new home he's planning to buy. Married men who are cheating on their wives seem to be particularly fond of taking unsuspecting targets to dream home environments where they invite the target to take part in an imaginary life together.

- Romantic Liars are also notorious for being difficult to reach when you want to find them. The reasons why should be fairly obvious. Married Romantic Liars, for example, have a built-in need to make certain you don't have a home telephone number for them. The same is true for a Romantic Liar who's given you a phony line about what he does for a living or where he works. If a guy is giving you the runaround about home or work numbers, tell him to get lost. If he claims he can't give you the numbers because he's an agent for the federal government, tell him you're the Queen of England.

- It's very characteristic of a Romantic Liar to exhibit signs of extreme mood swings to the point that he can go from a carefree, spontaneous pursuit of romance to an expression of despair in a matter of hours. Most victims of Romantic Deception characterize the relationship as one in which their partner eventually became very unpredictable in terms of mood or demeanor. The feeling that you're *walking on eggshells* around your partner is commonplace if you're involved with a Romantic Liar.

- Finally, Romantic Liars frequently engage in any number of potentially self-destructive behaviors. Although they're usually quite successful in hiding their reliance on drugs or alcohol in the beginning of a relationship, signs of drug and alcohol abuse usually crop up as time goes by.

The Forging of a Deceptive Relationship

Short of getting involved with someone you've known for the greater part of your life, there's no such thing as a fail-safe way to meet a potential partner. A Romantic Liar can come into your life from any direction, but yes, some settings are obviously more inviting of deceit than others. Chat rooms on the Internet, personal ads, and singles bars are obvious examples of where you're likely to encounter a dyed-in-the-wool Romantic Liar. But you can also meet a Romantic Liar at work, school, church, or through a friend who's just as clueless as you are about a potential partner's true character. More than one woman has ended up in a relationship with a Romantic Liar as a result of a blind date that was set up by a well-intentioned but totally-in-the-dark good friend.

A Romantic Liar's ability to forge a deceptive relationship begins with his ability to tell a *plausible* story and to tell it in a way that makes it *believable*. It doesn't make any difference whether he's lying about his marital status or his occupation or education or anything else, for that matter. It's his ability to tell a *plausible* story in a *believable* fashion that gives birth to a deceptive relationship. Many people mistakenly assume that a deceptive tale always has a fundamental element of implausibility or unbelievability and that there has to be something wrong with a woman who would fall for such a story to begin with. Nothing could be farther from the truth. All it takes for a long-term lie to be successful is that it be launched with the right amount of skill.

The Specific Stages of Deceptive Relationships

Every episode of Romantic Deception is unique, and there's no predicting just how long a deceptive relationship will last. The people involved vary from case to case, as do the settings in which the deception occurs and the lies that go into the overall misrepresentation. Despite the uniqueness of each case, though, there are certain stages you can expect a deceptive relationship to go through. From the first state to the last, the patterns are fairly predictable.

The First Stage

Deceptive relationships usually start off in a whirlwind. A new suitor arrives on the scene, and there's no mistake about it. He *is* a suitor, and an eager one at that. A Romantic Liar isn't the guy who shows only a passing interest in you. He's quite the opposite. If you're into being wined and dined, a Romantic Liar is the guy for you.

He sent flowers to my office after our first date, and then he started sending these cards. Every time I turned around he was doing something special— you know, some little sign of affection. I've had guys put the rush on me before, but he went overboard.

Gina, age 25

It was over the top from the beginning. It was like we had two dates and then we were an item.

Pamela, age 33

The Second Stage

Somewhere along the way—maybe a month, maybe two— your life starts to change. More than likely, though, you won't be sensitive to what's really going on. You'll be spending all your time together, but you'll also be spending all your time together *alone*—far away from the company of your friends and family. Little by little, significant elements of your life will undergo a transformation. If he's not calling you every few hours, he'll be in your physical presence. He might urge you to quit your job or drop your plans for school, or he might suggest you move in together. It's all happening so fast, but it seems to make so much sense, particularly in the context of all the passion and abundant romance that so characterizes deceptive relationships.

The really scary thing about all that was how I totally rearranged my life because of him. I'm almost embarrassed to admit it, but I dropped out of school because of Ted. I'm finally going back now, but I'd already be finished if I hadn't listened to him. Don't get me wrong. It was my decision. He wanted me to quit school, and I went along with it. That was my mistake.

Debbie, age 27

It was incredible. After about a week or ten days, it got to where we were never apart. I'd go to work, come home, and there he'd be. There were times I almost got to feeling a little suffocated; I should have paid attention to those feelings.

Claudia, age 38

At the second stage of a deceptive relationship, you're still relatively unsuspecting about the possibility of deception. You may have some hint that something isn't quite right about the relationship, but you're still a long way from acting on those feelings. Some of the danger signs can begin to surface at this stage, but the romance is still running full steam ahead. Chances are you'll have little opportunity to really get your true bearings.

Unfortunately, the second stage of a deceptive relationship is usually laced with as much romance as the first. Instead of paying attention to what is really going on, you're very likely to turn a blind eye.

The Third Stage

As long as you're involved with a Romantic Liar, you'll never be bored. The relationship *will* be exciting. The excitement that was there at the outset—the romantic dinners, great sex, and maybe even some adventurous vacations—has now been traded in for the excitement that goes along with your partner's unpredictability. The romance has been replaced by drama, and a different side of your partner is coming to light. If he's inclined toward alcohol or drug abuse, the lid is starting to come off, and now his mood swings are becoming more obvious. As they become more frequent, your uneasiness grows. You've started watching your own behavior closely, if only out of fear that you might set him off. By now he's criticizing you, your friends, and your family. Your uneasiness about the relationship is growing, but you don't know where to turn. The good times are still too good to give it up, so you stay committed. Your hope for the future clouds your judgment of the present. You're getting further and further entangled. Here's what you can expect in the third stage of a deceptive relationship:

- Feeling cut off from the rest of the world
- Feeling threatened or afraid of what your partner might do
- Sensing that your partner is checking up on you all of the time
- Feeling anxious about how the relationship is going
- Feeling that you are *walking on eggshells* around your partner
- Receiving criticism about your friends and family
- Sensing an effort to limit your contact with your friends and family
- Receiving criticism about your job, career, and future goals
- Receiving requests that you alter your appearance

The Fourth Stage

You'll know it when you reach the fourth stage of a deceptive relationship. You'll think you're losing your mind. By now the emotions are cascading down from all directions. Here's what the fourth stage of Romantic Deception is all about:

- Feeling depressed
- Feeling helpless
- Feeling that you have no control over your future
- Feeling that you doubt your own sanity
- Fearing what your partner might do if you left him
- Receiving verbal abuse from your partner
- Receiving physical abuse from your partner

Here's how one woman in the study described this stage of her relationship with a Romantic Liar.

> *I thought, I'm losing it—I'm losing it. Something he was doing or saying wouldn't make sense, so I'd try to deal with it. I'd ask him about it, but it would make things worse. He'd always have some kind of plausible explanation. Then I'd tell it to my friend and she would say 'Don't you remember—*

he said ABC not CBA.' Then I'd say, 'You're right.'
My friend would tell me, 'It's not you—it's him.'
He could take anything I said and twist it totally
around.

Nancy, age 28

The Fifth and Final Stage (Again and Again)

The last stage of a deceptive relationship begins when you make the decision to leave the relationship. Unfortunately, though, there's no telling how long the separation process will go on. As a rule, most women find it very difficult to totally disengage from a deceptive relationship on the first try. Deceptive relationships share much in common with other types of addictive relationships—they are classic expressions of the reward-punishment scenario—good times followed by bad followed by good. Denise, for example, took more than a year to end her relationship with Brad.

> *Over the next year, I probably tried to leave him four or five times. He'd always show up at my door and I'd take him back. Finally, I moved in the dead of night. I moved where he couldn't find me. I knew I had to get away from him where he couldn't keep coming back. I lost weight and I got real sick. I did a lot of reading. When I finally got a better job I was able to make a break.*

With all those negatives in play, why is it that every day there are thousands of women who end up in relationships with Romantic Liars? In other words, are there any characteristics of the women that predispose them to a relationship with a Romantic Liar in the first place? It all goes to the issue of vulnerability—the issue we'll look at next.

Vulnerability

I was totally devastated. I was humiliated. It never dawned on me that something like this could happen. Honesty was a real big deal to me—still is. But I guess I never expected somebody to just lie. It was horrible.

April, age 33

I grew up in a family where we were taught to tell the truth. My sisters and me—all of us are honest to a fault. The idea that somebody would make up all these stories was something that was foreign to my way of thinking. It just was.

Jamie, age 27

It never occurred to me to question what he told me. He said he was divorced; I believed him. What was I going to do—ask him to see the papers?

Joan, age 36

What you just read speaks volumes about the issue of vulnerability—why women fall victim to Romantic Liars in the first place. The same words also speak volumes about just how far off the mark the conventional wisdom really is when it comes to Romantic Deception.

Beware the Conventional Wisdom

The world of Romantic Deception is divided into two camps: the experienced and the uninitiated. Ask a victim what causes Romantic Deception and you'll get one set of answers. Ask someone in the ranks of the uninitiated and most likely you'll get a very different response.

Victims of Romantic Deception will readily tell you that there's no such thing as an easy answer when it comes to how or why a woman becomes a target. There aren't any easy answers when you want to know why women are vulnerable. Ask someone from the ranks of the uninitiated, though, and this is probably what you'll hear:

> *There's no way a woman could get involved in something like that without knowing what was going on.*

> *There's something inside women that make them vulnerable; they've got some need for men like that.*

> *There's no such thing as an unwilling victim.*

> *That's exactly what happens when a woman sits around waiting for Prince Charming.*

Statements like those are so commonplace that it's fair to say they constitute the *conventional wisdom* on the topic of Romantic Deception—the way the uninitiated are likely to view the world of Romantic Deception.

Unfortunately, statements like those are also very dangerous. For starters, statements like those aren't based on research; they're based on little more than unstated assumptions and delivered in a language that speaks of inner needs, unmet needs, dysfunctional environments, and all things psychological—words strung together in a language that puts all the emphasis on the victim and what she had to have done to get into such a mess to being with. What's missing, of course, is any discussion about the lying that goes on and the fact that one partner elects to lie to the other. The real travesty gets hidden and the blame is shifted. Instead of asking why some people choose to lie to others, all the talk is about the victim and what made her susceptible to the deception in the first place. The conventional wisdom is little more than *blaming the victim* dressed up in a cloak of psychological explanations.

The fact that there's a lot of *blaming the victim* that goes along with Romantic Deception shouldn't shock anyone. After all, *blaming the victim* is a strategy that allows people to feel comfortable, if nothing else. For people who adopt a *blaming the victim strategy,* there's a certain sense of security that follows, even if it's a false sense of security. As long as victims of Romantic Deception are seen as women who invited the deceit through their emotional insecurities or desperate life circumstances, the rest of the world remains protected (or so the rest of the world thinks). After all, *we* wouldn't be that insecure; *we* wouldn't be so desperate; *we* wouldn't close our eyes to something that was so obvious—or so the thinking goes.

There's no doubt in my mind that some women find comfort in logic like that. As I said before, there's a certain amount of security that would seem to follow when one adopts the conventional wisdom about Romantic Deception. Here's a case in point. It's a very instructive story—one passed along to me by my friend Maria.

The setting for this story was an informal dinner at Maria's home. Roger, Maria's friend of twenty-some-odd years, was there for dinner and some business discussion. At Maria's invitation, Roger brought along Tracey, the woman he'd been dating for the past year or so. Maria didn't know Tracey very well, but she'd met her on a couple of occasions. Maria believed that Tracey was very attached to Roger—maybe to the point that Tracey had marriage on her mind.

On the other hand, Maria knew Roger like the back of her hand. More than just business acquaintances, Maria and Roger had been friends for more than two decades, and Maria would be the first to tell you that there were no secrets between them. As Maria said while leading into the story, *I know Roger's first wife, his second wife, his two children, and his secretary. I even know the two mistresses he had during his first marriage.* Maria also knew that Roger was still the same philanderer he'd always been. He'd been dating Tracey for nearly a year, but he was still very involved with Catherine, the woman he'd been carrying on with for more than four years.

Roger was tending the steaks on the grill and Maria went to check on the progress. Since Tracey wasn't around, Maria took the opportunity to engage in a little playful grilling of Roger. *Have you bothered to tell Tracey about Catherine?* she asked. Roger knew Maria well enough to take no offense at the question, and he also knew he could speak the truth. *No,* Roger said, *and I don't see any reason to. What she doesn't know won't hurt her.* Maria also knew Roger well enough to just let his remark go by without comment. After all, it really wasn't any of her business. Maria went inside to put the finishing touches on the dinner table.

Somewhere midway through the dinner, Maria mentioned my research and the book I was writing. Since Maria had read some of the draft material on the manuscript, she started lacing the conversation with examples of cases I'd uncovered during the research. Maria was really doing most of the talking, but Tracey eventually jumped headlong into the conversation.

Tracey was very certain of how she viewed Romantic Deception. *Why that's impossible,* Tracey blurted out. *There's just no way a woman could get involved in a relationship like that and not know what was going on. There's no way.* That was Tracey's opinion—the long and short of it and straight to the point.

To this day Maria doesn't know what prompted Roger to do what he did, but Roger took exception to what Tracey had just said. In so many words, he said he really wasn't certain Tracey knew what she was talking about. As a matter of fact, Roger looked Tracey straight in the eyes and came out with a fairly straight-up sort of question: *How do you know I'm not cheating on you?*

According to Maria, Tracey didn't spend even a second to think about her response. She just answered Roger with all the conviction you could imagine. *I'd just know it*, Tracey said. *I just would. There's no way you could be cheating on me without me knowing it.* Then, with an all-knowing quality to her voice, Tracey added: *Good grief, Roger, you don't have enough time to be cheating on me!*

Roger didn't say a word and neither did Maria. They also had the good sense to refrain from winking, grinning, or kicking one another under the table. At last report, Roger was still carrying on with both Catherine and Tracey, and there was no evidence that Tracey had a clue about what was really going on.

Maria knows the truth; I know the truth; and now you and thousands of other folks know the truth. The one person who apparently still doesn't know the truth is Tracey. But remember: Tracey is certain a woman would know if she were in a deceptive relationship. If nothing else, I suspect Tracey feels very safe. For Tracey, vulnerability isn't even an issue.

※

Because the conventional wisdom on Romantic Deception would have us believe it's something that only happens to emotionally vulnerable women, I decided to take a closer look and question the women I was interviewing on that very point. In particular, I wanted to know about their life circumstances when they met the men who ultimately proved to be Romantic Liars.

To say that there was significant variation in their circumstances hardly captures how much diversity I discovered. I encountered a lot of women who willingly admitted they got involved while they were still on the rebound from a divorce or the termination of a significant relationship. But I also encountered far more who described their circumstances in terms that were largely positive. Because so much of the conventional wisdom about Romantic Deception suggests that it's something that only happens to desperate women looking for a caretaker of some sort, it's very instructive to consider what some of the women actually told me. For example:

> I was twenty-six years old when this happened. I'd finished school and I'd spent two years living in Europe. I came back to the States, got my career going, and I was totally happy. Twenty-six was the best year of my life, until I got involved with him.
>
> **Simone, age 29**

> I wasn't desperate or in a panic to get married or anything like that. I really liked what I was doing and I loved where I was living. I had an active social life and I was dating a couple of different guys. Everything was going great.
>
> **Beth, age 26**

> It had been about five years since my divorce, but I was pretty content with how my life was going. Yeah. Pretty content. My kids were out of the nest, I was getting into my career again, and I was pretty satisfied with my life.
>
> **Stacey, age 42**

> Three words? Settled, happy, and I had direction.
>
> **Bonnie, age 31**

In the face of words like those, it's difficult to put a lot of faith in the conventional wisdom about Romantic Deception, at least the part that suggests it is something that only happens to women in dire emotional straits. The notion that all victims of Romantic Deception are drawn into deceptive relationships as a result of their insecurities or inner needs or desperate life circumstances just doesn't hold water. Factors like that might explain *some* cases of Romantic Deception, but they obviously don't explain all of them.

If it's time to discard a good amount of the conventional wisdom, where do we turn when we want to understand why so many women are vulnerable to Romantic Deception? As a start, I would suggest discarding the question altogether. Instead of asking what makes women vulnerable to Romantic Deception, I would suggest we look at what factors in our society in general make deception possible in the first place. When that's the question we ask, we get some very different answers.

The Truth Bias

The idea that people are who and what they say they are is merely an assumption. It's not only a common assumption, it's a necessary assumption. It's what some have referred to as the *truth bias* that operates in society—an implicit assumption that unless we're shown some reason to believe otherwise, we generally believe we're being told the truth. You can think of the truth bias as a societal default position—the way we'll normally operate unless we get a signal to act differently.

All of us probably know some people who are highly skeptical and cynical about life in general, but I suspect even those folks manage to muster some level of truth bias in their day-to-day activities. If they didn't, they wouldn't get much done. Just imagine what life would be like if we didn't operate with a truth bias, and how society would function without it. The sight of everyone running around fact-checking and verifying everything they were told is a bit incomprehensible. To say that it would be a society of paranoids with all of us at the brink of insanity would be an understatement.

In other words, some measure of truth bias is necessary if our society is to function smoothly and efficiently. It shouldn't surprise us, then, to learn that Romantic Deception is partly fueled by the truth bias of the larger social order. It was apparent in any number of the interviews.

> *You know it never occurred to me that anybody would lie like that. I can look back on it now and realize there wasn't much he told me that was the truth. But that didn't even occur to me at the time. I'm just not like that. I don't expect people to lie to me. I expect them to tell the truth.*

Katie, age 19

> *I felt really stupid. I had no reason to doubt anything he said or did. We'd probably been together for four or five months before I had any hint anything was wrong. Up to that point, I trusted him completely. I didn't have any reason to doubt him, so I didn't.*

Jerri, age 41

> *The thing about him was that he told me that honesty was something that was real important to him. He told me he'd been hurt real bad by this woman that lied to him. I believed him. It's as simple as that. He told me he thought it was important to be honest and I figured he was telling the truth. Boy was I fooled.*

Ellie, age 33

> *How the hell are you supposed to know? Are you supposed to have this attitude that every guy you will meet is lying? You'd go nuts if you did that.*

Lydia, age 40

Socialization

As much as the *truth bias* is imbedded in society, socialization is imbedded in us as individuals. It's the process of socialization that gives us the cultural knowledge we need if we're to function as a member of society. At times we rail against it, but it's with us, in us, and around us from cradle to grave.

As children, we were taught about the importance of honesty and why it's important to tell the truth. If the process works the way it's supposed to, we'll tell the truth because it's the right thing to do. In a word, we will have *internalized* the value. The value of honesty and truth-telling will become such a part of us that we don't give it a moment's thought.

When values are internalized, they become part of our core belief structure, defining who we are in the most fundamental and important sense. And our internalized values also function as our internal compass—letting us know when behavior (ours or someone else's) is out of bounds. Unfortunately, our core beliefs have a way of becoming so important to us that it's often very difficult to imagine that we could even find ourselves in the company of someone who didn't hold the same values.

Much like the horror that the neighbors usually express when they learn that the man next door has just been nabbed for being a serial murderer, it's very difficult for well-socialized truth tellers to even contemplate that they could be mixed up with a big-time liar. And that's the whole point about socialization and how it gives rise to deceptive relationships. Ask me who's vulnerable to Romantic Deception, and high on my list will be the woman who was *raised right*. Show me a woman who believes in honesty and I'll show you a woman who finds it hard to even imagine that she could get mixed up with a big-time liar. Show me a woman who places a premium on honesty in a relationship, and I'll show you a vulnerable target.

Apart from the socialization that takes place to define our core beliefs, there's also a hefty amount of gender definition that works to increase our vulnerabilities. From a very young age we're taught and shown and told how to behave if we're to be seen as attractive. The messages hit us early, and they hit us from all sides—parents, teachers, movies, and magazines. If that's not enough, there's television, popular songs, peer groups, and billboards. When the process of socialization works, we get the message.

Part of the message has to do with *good behavior* in social situations—not just what to wear or how to dress, but how to be polite. We learn what's expected of us on the job and on a date. It's all part of the larger social order. So many of the rules of the social order are so inconsequential that we rarely give them much thought, yet the rules so frequently govern our behavior. And sometimes it's the rules that end up getting us in trouble. When you hear the words of women who've been down the road of deceit, it's hard to argue against the power of the larger social order. You get a sense of how powerful the forces of socialization can be.

> *I guess I grew up with this idea that I was supposed to be all nice and polite. So you meet some guy and he starts telling you he's this and that. What are you supposed to do? Do you just say 'prove it'?*

Patsy, age 35

> *Sometimes I think the whole dating thing would work a lot better if we quit being so nice. Imagine what that would be like. Some guy asks you out and you tell him you need his home phone number first. Some guy wants you to go to dinner and you tell him you'll need to meet him at his office to see if he really works where he says he works. Some guy tells you he's divorced and you tell him you'll need to see the papers. Yeah. That would be a good one. But it's true. We shouldn't be so polite.*

Anita, age 41

The Myths

Finally, I'm convinced a lot of our vulnerability to Romantic Deception stems from how Romantic Liars are portrayed in the media. Given what I know about Romantic Deception as a result of my research, and given the way the phenomenon is usually presented in the media, I'm left to conclude there's a wide gulf between the two. It's safe to say that the popular media's presentation of the topic is largely mythical.

Just think about it for a minute. How many television movies have you seen about Romantic Deception? Quite a few, I suspect. And you've probably read a novel or two with the same sort of theme. Even the news media carries an occasional story about a case of Romantic Deception—often a story that involves a wealthy woman being duped out of a mountain of money.

There's no question that tales of Romantic Deception, whether in print or on the screen, grab our interest. Unfortunately, though, the public accounts—the ones that make it into the mainstream media—have subtly created a host of myths about Romantic Deception. The myths, in turn, lead to a string of mistaken assumptions about what Romantic Liars are really like and how the game of Romantic Deception is played. It's the mistaken assumptions that make a lot of women vulnerable.

To understand how this happens, think about a typical made-for-television movie that revolves around the theme of Romantic Deception. Chances are the male lead (the Romantic Liar who's eventually found out) will be a drop-dead handsome, charismatic charmer who's portrayed as living life in the fast lane with some equally fast lane sort of women. If he's not wealthy enough on his own to support two or three entire families at once, he'll be bilking some wealthy woman out of all she has.

The story may be a totally fictionalized account or it may be loosely based on actual events. It makes no difference. The story will be laced with a lot of glitz, a fair amount of glamour, some high drama, and usually a lot of intrigue. It's very easy to be drawn into the story, at least to the point of following it all the way through. But it's also easy to conclude that the story was a little extreme. Indeed, I suspect that thousands of women have watched the same movies or read the same accounts and come to the same conclusion—something like that could never happen to *me. Interesting story, but I don't have enough money to attract the attention of a con artist. Interesting story, but I don't live life in the fast lane with men like that all around me.* And that's where part of the vulnerability to deception starts. It's when we make the assumption that what we've watched or read about is *a little too extreme* or *a little too far outside our realm of experience* that we make our first mistake.

Romantic Deception frequently does involve some extreme elements, but most of the cases I researched were actually rather mundane in their content. They involved real women going about their lives in a work-a-day world—not wealthy heiresses or jet-setting career women. They also involved some fundamentally ordinary men who chose to re-create their identities.

Yes, I had some spectacular cases that came my way when I started looking for women to interview. For example, I had limited contact with a woman who discovered her partner was featured on a national television show about high-profile criminals who were on the run. As it turned out, the man she was dating had murdered his wife (maybe that's what he really meant to say when he said he was no longer married). At any rate, the victim in this case wanted me to pay her money for the interview. I couldn't, so I didn't get all the details. I'm sure the story had a lot of high drama and intrigue, but I'm also certain it was an extreme case.

The truth is that the majority of the cases I heard about were the sort that would never make it to the screen, the printed page, or the local news broadcast. And therein lies the problem. The media is giving a lot of women a pretty distorted view of what Romantic Deception is all about. As I mentioned before, all Romantic Liars are not middle-aged, married men in the throes of a midlife crisis. All Romantic Liars are not high-rolling, *life-in-the-fast-lane* characters who have the resources to maintain two or more households. Quite a few Romantic Liars are single, and age—like apparent financial resources—is absolutely no predictor of whether or not a man is an imposter.

Another common myth is the notion that a Romantic Liar will be a captivating man with the social skills of a diplomat and the good looks of a screen idol. *Drop-dead handsome; suave; sophisticated*—just some of the words you'd probably hear if you asked most people to describe a Romantic Liar. As it turned out, the men I heard about in the interviews were acceptable, to be sure, at least to the point that the women were willing to give the relationship a chance. But I didn't hear story after story about men who could cause a room to go silent with their mere presence. There were a few stories about men who were described as exceptionally good-looking, but the majority of the men I heard about were only mildly attractive or even nondescript.

Finally, if the stories I collected are any indication, most cases of Romantic Deception don't involve confidence games in the traditional sense. Romantic Deception may involve an emotional con, but a financial swindle isn't necessarily involved. Yes, I heard a few cases about attempted financial swindles of one sort or another, but the majority of cases didn't have the true confidence game quality. Now that's not to say that there aren't a host of con artists operating out there. It's just that a Romantic Liar is not necessarily a con artist out to take your money.

The bottom line is that you run a great risk when you pay too much attention to the way Romantic Liars are portrayed in the media. If you figure you could never be a target because you don't live life in the fast lane or you don't have the resources to capture the interest of a con artist, you owe it to yourself to think again. I dare say the typical Romantic Liar, if there is such a creature, is very different from how most people would picture him. The lesson is a simple one. If you believe the myths, you're vulnerable.

SECTION II

The Lies They Tell

Two strategies are involved in nearly all cases of deception. On the one hand, there's deception for the purpose of concealment—lies and misrepresentations designed to keep secrets and hide the truth. On the other hand, there is deception to create an illusion—the use of lies and misrepresentation to foster a false impression or illusion.

When the concealment strategy is in play, you can expect a lot of lies of omission—a liar's deliberate failure to mention important facts or bits of information about his life. When it's the illusion strategy in play, the emphasis will be on lies of commission—a liar's deliberate misstatement of fact.

In the real world, of course, it doesn't make much sense to spend a lot of time worrying about which kind of strategy's in use or what general type of lie is being perpetrated. It also makes little sense to try to predict what kind of lie a Romantic Liar will tell in what kind of situation—it might be one sort of lie here and a totally different sort of lie there.

The key—at least in the case of Romantic Deception—is whether or not you can identify potential lies and misrepresentations when you encounter them. Unfortunately, that isn't always as easy as it might sound.

When a Romantic Liar is successful in his deception, it's largely because he's told lies that have a high degree of *plausibility* and *believability*, at least for a while. As I mentioned in an earlier section, Romantic Liars have a way of telling lies that *could be true* (the *plausibility* component), and they tell them in a way that makes them *believable* (the *believability* component). In many cases, long-running deception only comes to light when a Romantic Liar crosses the line and enters the world of lies that are a little too implausible. In other cases, the deception only comes to light by mere chance. Until the line of implausibility is crossed or the forces of chance converge to expose the truth, however, many Romantic Liars are able to get away with their deception for weeks, months, or even years.

Romantic Liars are largely successful because their lies have these two essential components—*believability* and *plausibility*. This concept is central to any understanding of what really goes on in the world of deceptive relationships. For many people— particularly those who've never been on the receiving end of a big-time lie—the idea that someone could lie and get away with it is simply too much to comprehend. Not understanding how plausibility and believability combine to produce successful deception, many people fall back on the conventional wisdom you read about earlier—the assumption that says it takes some sort of fool to be fooled by a Romantic Liar.

Of course the really curious element in that sort of thinking is how so many of the same people are unwilling to apply the same sort of thinking when it comes to deception in other circumstances. What comes to mind here is a recent case of deception that made national headlines, largely because of some of the individuals involved in the twisted tale. It's a story I'm always fond of telling, particularly when I'm talking to someone who's steadfast in his or her belief that there's no such thing as an innocent victim in cases of Romantic Deception. The story has absolutely nothing to do with dating or romance or anything else along those lines. It does, however, have a lot to do with big-time deception.

The story involves a man by the name of Joseph Yandle. In the early 1970s, Yandle was convicted and given a life sentence for his part in an armed robbery. Yandle was the driver of the getaway car. The real tragedy in this tale, some would say, was the fact that Yandle, a two-tour Vietnam veteran who saw some of the war's worst action, returned to the United States with a serious heroin addiction. A winner of the Bronze Star and two Purple Hearts, Yandle had an addiction that fueled his need for money. That, in turn, drove him to take part in the robbery, where an innocent liquor store clerk lost his life.

In prison, Yandle's life began to turn around. He organized the other veterans for a counseling program, and he also organized a *Toys for Tots* Christmas campaign from inside the prison walls. Earning a college degree while behind bars, Yandle became a model prisoner to the point that he eventually attracted the attention of no less a journalist than Mike Wallace. Once Wallace's interview with the decorated veteran hit the airwaves, the wheels started turning. Veterans groups organized; they promoted the cause of Yandle; they lobbied to get him out of prison. Finally, in 1995, the Massachusetts governor, William Weld, commuted Yandle's sentence. The one-time heroin addict was a free man.

But shortly afterwards, the truth came to light. Joseph Yandle had been in the Army, to be sure, but he'd never spent one day in Vietnam, let alone two heroic tours. He was, in a word or two, not the man he claimed he was. He was an imposter of the first order, and he managed to fool quite a few folks. It was merely by chance that the Yandle story came to the attention of someone who decided to take a closer look at his background.

I find it hard to believe that a journalist of Mike Wallace's caliber and a successful politician like the former governor were willing victims—caught up in the glory or heroics to the point that they were willing to believe anything. I also find it hard to believe that they were driven by *some inner need* to be deceived to the point that they closed their eyes. In point of fact, both men—Wallace and Weld—had nothing to gain by being taken in; indeed, they had everything to lose. I suspect it was the *believability* and the *plausibility* of the lie that fooled them.

And that's the way it is with a lot of Romantic Liars. They tell lies that are very *plausible,* and they tell them in ways that make them *believable*. It's as simple as that—people telling lies in such a way that most people don't bother to really check them out.

Since a truly practiced Romantic Liar can go for weeks, or months, or even years without a serious slip-up, about the only thing you can do to protect yourself is to remain alert to all the different sorts of lies a Romantic Liar might tell. Some people would tell you that you can train yourself to carefully monitor body language and facial expressions, and thereby pick up on clues to deceit, but I'm not a big believer in that school of thought. I'm also not a big believer in the school of thought that says you can train yourself to use certain interrogation techniques to sniff out a liar early on. Some people might be able to school themselves in those areas, but I'd never say it's a sure bet.

My personal opinion is that catching a Romantic Liar usually takes more than a little bit of time and effort. If you want to catch a Romantic Liar you first have to know where to look. In other words, you first have to know what he's apt to lie about. In the next few pages, you'll be reading about all sorts of lies that Romantic Liars have come up with.

To bring some order to the picture, I've classified the many different misrepresentations I've heard about by *type of lie—availability, status, explanatory, personal tragedy,* and *the just-plain-crazy lie*. Though you might think those categories would pretty much cover the gamut, I'm not about to suggest they do. I've interviewed too many women who've been on the receiving end of too many lies to think I've heard them all. If nothing else, Romantic Liars are very inventive. I'm convinced there's probably a new type of lie born every day. At a minimum, though, learning about the types of lies I've defined might cause you to start thinking in a more critical and objective fashion, particularly if any of the lies sound familiar.

Availability Lies

He told me he had to go out of town and I thought it was just another one of his business trips. I was used to that. I knew he traveled all the time, at least that's what he'd told me. Then he didn't come back. I finally called his office, and the secretary told me he went home to be with his wife and kids for the holidays. That's how I found out he was married.

Sherry, age 28

It was about seven o'clock in the morning and I heard this awful banging on the door downstairs. I didn't even get the door open when she came storming in. Here was this strange woman crashing in through the front door. I was scared to death. It was David's wife. I swear I didn't have any idea he was married. He told me he was divorced. He even told me his ex-wife was this horrible, alcoholic, crazy woman. He made her sound like a shrew. She wasn't. I know she wasn't 'cause we talked a long time. God I was embarrassed.

Candy, age 24

Of all the lying that goes on in the world of Romantic Deception, it's the lies about availability that seem to be the most common. When a Romantic Liar tells an availability lie, he's misrepresenting the extent to which he's really available for a relationship.

As you might expect, a married man's efforts to convince you he's single top the list when it comes to availability lies. Of all the lying and misrepresentation I heard about in the interviews, the charades in that category were the most numerous. Here are a couple of examples, each quite typical of the sort of lying and misrepresentation that actually go on.

Barbara is still a little unclear just how Martin was able to pull it off. When they met, Martin was living in a small town about ninety miles away. Like so many other cases of Romantic Deception, theirs was a whirlwind sort of romance. If Martin wasn't in town to see Barbara (something he managed every few days and nights), they were on the phone together. If Barbara wasn't calling Martin at home, he was calling her. Their plans for the future quickly took shape.

With Martin wrapping up the last of his father's estate and selling off the substantial land holdings, the future looked bright. Martin would leave the small town he disliked so much and he could, as he put it, *close that chapter* in his life. He would be able to open that business he'd been planning, and the two of them could start fresh.

As to Martin's former life—the life he'd led before he met Barbara—there was only one word for it: *noble*. He'd managed a successful career prior to returning home to care for aging parents, and he'd also single-handedly raised a fine son— something he was forced to do when a totally unfit wife and mother abandoned Martin and their infant son less than two years into their marriage.

It wasn't that Barbara was totally without suspicion. Indeed, it was when her suspicions finally got the best of her that one of her friends recommended that she talk to me. As you'll soon learn, it was probably a good thing that we did talk. Martin was hardly the guy he made himself out to be.

Apparently it was of no consequence to Martin that Barbara ordered the wedding dress shortly after he proposed and they set the date, and he didn't mind being introduced to all of Barbara's friends as the man she was going to marry. Martin also had no trouble fending off Barbara's inquiries when she asked him why she hadn't really met any of his friends. He responded to that question the same way he responded to just about any question Barbara had about his present circumstances—*that* (whatever the topic might be) *was a chapter in my life that I'm closing out.*

Like all stories of Romantic Deception, Barbara's is a long and complicated one, so much so that it's worthy of a book in its own right. If we fast-forward to the end, though, this is what we come to learn. First, Martin was still very married and living at home with his wife. To this day Barbara isn't certain how she could have made so many telephone calls to his home without his wife finding out. And Barbara still has no idea how Martin planned to pull off two marriages at one time. Second, Martin's house was not only home to a wife, it was home to two young daughters (something Barbara only learned several weeks after our initial conversation). Finally, Martin had misrepresented virtually every important aspect of his life history. You name it, and Martin embellished or fabricated it—education, work history, and military career.

While Barbara's story is instructive on many fronts, the single most important misrepresentation—his claim of being a divorced man who'd raised a son to adulthood—was the one that set the stage for all that followed. He started with an availability lie and then he filled in the blanks.

It goes without saying, of course, that much of the deception in Barbara's case was made possible by the fact that Martin was living out of town. On the other hand, deception that's based on an availability lie can happen when a Romantic Liar lives right across town or just a few blocks away. One of the stories you read about in the introductory section is a good case in point.

⚜

Carole, you may recall, found herself in a skyrocketing romance with Bill—a romance that went on for months, even though Bill married another woman shortly after he met Carole. It's reasonable to ask how on earth something like that is possible. Like Barbara's story, Carole's is a long and involved one, but here are the elements that made the deception work for Bill. All you need is the outline to see how it worked.

First, the woman Bill married was a nurse who worked the three-to-eleven shift, so Bill was free to court Carole most any evening, just so long as he made it back home by the time his wife arrived (usually a little before midnight). Second, when Carole first met Bill (a couple of weeks before his marriage to the other woman), he introduced her to his roommate, Art. Carole thought Art was one of the most disgusting human beings she had ever met. Since everything about Art offended her (from his personal hygiene to his language), Carole was quite content for her romance with Bill to take place at her apartment.

As for Art, he was more than willing to assist Bill in his charade. When Bill got married, he simply left his answering machine with Art at the apartment. Bill was an especially attentive sort, to the point that Carole rarely had reason to call him. And Art was apparently very dutiful in getting Carole's messages to Bill if she did call to talk to him.

It was only a series of chance circumstances that caused Carole's relationship with Bill to end, but when it did, it didn't just unravel—it came apart at the seams. Not only did Carole discover that Bill was married, she also discovered that he wasn't an attorney. As it turned out, Bill was a customer order clerk who worked at the service desk at that large manufacturing plant. To this day Carole would probably tell you that Bill presented a very believable image, particularly when he squired Carole all over the facilities one weekend. Not only did he introduce her to all the workers, he took her upstairs to the fifth floor to show her his office—despite the fact that he actually worked at the customer service desk just a step or two above the basement.

❧

Carole's story of deception, like Barbara's, began with her boyfriend's misrepresentation of his availability. While it's technically true that Bill was single when he and Carole first met and began dating, it's difficult to excuse Bill's behavior on the basis of a technicality. Bill's lie came in the form of a lie of omission. He just kept his mouth shut about the fact that he was engaged and that he got married. The lie remained alive, at least in part, because his friend Art was a willing accomplice. Throw into the equation the factor of a wife's schedule that made it fairly easy for Bill to carry on, and there you have it—a married man parading around like he's single, even though he's living with a wife right across town. And even all of that doesn't begin to capture the full extent of Bill's lying. After all, in Bill we had a fellow who was even willing to drag his girlfriend into an office that wasn't his—all in an effort to convince her he was an up-and-coming attorney.

Sad commentaries on the way life gets lived, but stories like the ones you just read are so common that they constitute something akin to a cultural fixture in our society—the sort of thing that's the centerpiece in everything from novels to movies to popular humor. Like I said, the stories of married men posing as single, divorced, or otherwise totally available top the list when it comes to availability lies.

Though not as common, there were a few stories I collected that were similar enough to one another that I'm inclined to think they probably constitute still another theme in the world of availability lies. Each of these stories involved a man claiming he'd recently been engaged or otherwise involved in a long-term relationship.

All the stories shared three things in common. First, the previous relationship (the engagement or the long-term involvement) was painted in a very favorable light. Second, the details of the breakup were sketchy to the point that you would have to use your imagination as to what really took place. Finally, each of the stories proved to be false, at least in some significant way.

In one case, for example, Judy found out that John's involvement and eventual breakup with Ann (his former partner) was anything but the way he had made it out to be. Judy had been operating on the assumption that John was a pretty decent guy. He'd been engaged to a really great gal (or so he said), but the engagement ended when his fiancée eventually opted for graduate school instead of marriage.

He also left the strong impression on Judy that he'd been pretty noble about what happened—even going so far as to tell Judy that he didn't think it was right to stand in the way of his fiancée's career if it was that important to her. Despite the picture he had painted, the truth about John came out. Eventually Judy's relationship with John deteriorated to the point that she went looking for answers. That's when she tracked down Ann and learned the truth.

Ann's side of the story was very different. Yes, she had been involved with John, but they were never engaged. Like Judy, Ann had found herself on the receiving end of some of John's tirades—explosions that eventually reached the level of physical violence. Ann told Judy she was lucky to find out what John was really like when she did, adding that she'd wasted fourteen months of her life on him. Then telling Judy that she'd be happy to share (just in the spirit of sisterhood), Ann offered to fax Judy a copy of the restraining order she had on John. It's safe to say that John had a reason for telling the story in the way he did.

There's no telling exactly why John chose to fabricate the story about his engagement to Ann, but we can certainly speculate. Maybe it was just too good a lie to pass up. Think of what it accomplished. First, it signaled that John wasn't afraid of commitment (*after all, he'd been engaged, or so he said*). Second, it signaled that he was an acceptable sort of guy (*after all, another woman found him acceptable enough to accept his proposal, or so he said*). Finally, it sent the message that he was an understanding sort of guy (*after all, he was willing to step aside in favor of his fiancée's career*).

None of this is to suggest that every guy you meet who tells you he just broke up with his fiancée or long-time significant other is telling you a lie. Thousands of relationships come to an end in a peaceful, mature way every day. On the other hand, thousands of breakups end in ways that are anything but healthy. Somebody goes psycho and all hell breaks loose. When that's the way it goes, and assuming it's the guy who went ballistic, he has any number of reasons why he wouldn't want you to know what really happened. Sometimes it pays to be suspicious of a potential partner, even when he seems so downright decent.

Status Lies

He told me he had gone to the University of Missouri and then he got an M.B.A. from the University of Illinois. He also told me he had this great house in Clearwater he was using as rental property. I tell you what else—he was always talking about his family like they were real wealthy and how they always put pressure on him to do this and that. I guess he just wanted me to think he was a bigshot or something.

It's when the stuff about his job didn't make sense that I decided to check him out. I found this service on the Internet that checks out people. Turns out he'd never been to the University of Missouri or Illinois. And we couldn't find any property in his

*name in Clearwater. I imagine that stuff about his
parents was made-up, too, but I don't know. The
education thing, though—that was definitely a lie.*

Belinda, age 31

Close behind the availability lie, at least as far as how often
they're told, are status lies—all of the misrepresentations
a Romantic Liar makes to enhance his position in life. Taking
their cues from what society defines as desirable, Romantic Liars
frequently inflate all sorts of status attributes—education,
occupation, income or wealth, social connections, and even athletic prowess.

If the results of my study are any indication, the lies and misrepresentations about educational credentials top the list of status lies. Not only do many Romantic Liars inflate the amount of
education they actually have, but they frequently embellish their
academic records with claims that they attended the nation's
more prestigious universities.

When it comes to academic degrees, misrepresentations
about graduate degrees, short of the Ph.D. degree, are most
common. For example, M.B.A. degrees seem to be the degree of
choice among Romantic Liars—at least those who opt for
a phony graduate degree—but master's degrees in psychology
also seem quite popular. Some Romantic Liars appear to be
content to limit themselves to a bachelor's degree, but they frequently claim they attended the nation's more prestigious
universities.

I suspect the educational misrepresentations are so common
simply because they're so easy to execute. All a Romantic Liar has
to do is let the words come out of his mouth. Unless he's chal-
lenged on the claim in some way, who's to know he's lying? An
educational status lie might be a problem in the workplace, particularly if somebody's supposed to have technical skills that
match up with a degree, but a dating or intimate relationship is a
very different situation.

If there's any good news about the fact that so many people seem to be wandering around with phony educational claims, it's this: Educational credentials are usually very easy to verify. All it usually takes is one phone call. What's more, educational lies frequently play a central role in a Romantic Liar's overall web of deceit. Once you spot an educational lie, there's a better than even chance that it will lead you to other lies as well. For example, educational lies are often used to shore up phony occupational claims, and they can also serve a Romantic Liar well if he's trying to explain away his past (as in covering over a previous marriage by telling you *I was a graduate student at Rutgers in the early '90s*).

As for phony occupational claims, most Romantic Liars will just claim to have higher-status occupations than they actually have. For example, the electrician's apprentice tells you he's an electrical engineer, or the customer service representative tells you he's the manager of marketing and distribution.

Some Romantic Liars, however, take it a step farther by using all sorts of props and settings to enhance the validity of their occupational claims. Renee, for example, has yet to figure out who was on the other end of the line when Todd was taking all those calls on his cell phone. At the time the calls were coming in, all the talk of business deals, business meetings, and business lunches made perfect sense. After all, Todd was the town's premier executive recruiter, or so he said. As it turned out, Todd was about as far from being an executive recruiter as he could be. Instead of pretending he found jobs for other people, Todd should have been trying to get his own job. There's no question he needed one. For the five months he was with Renee, Todd had been unemployed and living off of credit cards.

Chad's misrepresentation, on the other hand, matched Todd's charade and then some. His claim to fame was his position as a real-estate investor, and he had the posh office to prove it. He also had a telephone, a fax, and a copy machine, along with copies of the *Wall Street Journal* and all sorts of real-estate brochures stacked up on his desk. The couple of times Linda met Chad at his office, the setting looked genuine enough. In fact, everything about Chad seemed genuine for about three months. Then the truth came out. Chad was the maintenance man for the building where he claimed he had his office. Apparently he simply decided to appropriate a vacant office on the top floor and use it to enhance his image.

Where phony educational and occupational credentials leave off, claims of substantial wealth and social connection begin. Neil, for example, led Jessica to believe that he was very well-connected in social and political circles, going so far as to tell her that several of the local businessmen were trying to talk him into running for the city council. Since Jessica later found out that almost everything Neil told her about himself was a lie, she concluded he was lying about all his social connections, too. I leave it up to you to make your own judgment, but Jessica's reasoning sounds pretty solid to me.

> I had him checked out. Well I guess it was really my sister, Celeste, who had him checked out. She thought there was something wrong from the very first. When she started looking into his background, Neil and I were already history. I guess she just wanted to help me get over it—you know—show me what a real wacko he was. She found out all sorts of stuff—an ex-wife he hadn't told me about and how he filed for bankruptcy about five years ago. He'd also been nailed for hot checks. There's no way he was going to run for office.

Certainly most of the status lies I learned about had to do with the more traditional status variables of education, occupation, and income, but that's not to say Romantic Liars don't venture into other areas of status misrepresentation as well. For example, false claims of athletic prowess are actually fairly common. Among the interviews was one account of a Romantic Liar who falsely claimed to have played on a nationally ranked university basketball team (noting, in fact, that his team made it to the prestigious Final Four Basketball Tournament). Another claimed he had been the quarterback for the Louisiana State University football team. Still another claimed to have played professional football in the National Football League until, alas, he blew out his knee. All the stories turned out to be false from start to finish.

Less common, but certainly important, would be the misrepresentation about religious affiliation or involvement. There was only one misrepresentation along those lines that turned up in my interviews, but it deserves mention if for no other reason than it once again demonstrates that there is apparently no topic too sacred for a Romantic Liar. The case that came to my attention in this regard involved Margaret, a woman who'd spent approximately two years in a convent as a young woman.

Although she eventually left the convent, she retained a strong faith in Catholicism. For her, a man's religious affiliation and level of involvement were exceptionally important considerations when it came to choosing a life partner. Throughout their courtship and up to the time of their marriage, Dale claimed to be a practicing Catholic. Indeed, there were times during their courtship when Dale chastised Margaret because she had missed confession a time or two.

To say that Dale did a hundred-and-eighty-degree turn at the altar would be an understatement. The first sign that something was wrong was Dale's verbal abuse, directed toward Margaret for no apparent reason. Within weeks, though, Dale was becoming physically abusive, despite the fact that Margaret was pregnant with their first child. With her strong religious background and a baby on the way, Margaret found herself with few options and an overwhelming sense of betrayal. She thought she had married a practicing Catholic, and she had a set of assumptions about what that meant. But Dale was as far from being a practicing Catholic as anything she could have imagined. It was only after years of deception that Dale admitted it had been a good ten years since he had seen the inside of a confessional.

❦

Finally, there are cases of status misrepresentation involving sexuality. The classic example of this would be a man who hides his bisexuality while pursuing a relationship with a woman. Less extreme, perhaps, but no less important, would be cases in which a Romantic Liar has certain unconventional sexual interests he keeps secret from his partner. Among the interviews was one such case—one that involved Craig, a cross-dresser.

The story of Becky's involvement with Craig takes on an interesting dimension if for no other reason than Craig's totally macho appearance and behavior. To hear Becky tell it, Craig had the body of a professional weight lifter, and he was never known to pass up a chance to drink beer with his buddies when they left their construction jobs after a particularly rough day. Indeed, Becky once told him early in their dating that he was so good-looking that she found it hard to believe some woman hadn't snatched him up already. In fact, she playfully followed up her remark with a question as to whether he was *gay or something like that.* Maintaining his macho demeanor, Craig responded with a hearty *not on your life!*

Apparently Craig was satisfied that he had truthfully answered Becky's inquiry when he spoke those words with all the conviction in the world. And I guess, in a technical sense, he had. I say that because Becky eventually learned that Craig was a cross-dresser. Before the truth came out, Becky agonized for weeks as her intuition told her something just wasn't right with the relationship. For Becky, Craig's late-night and unexplained whereabouts only made sense if she allowed herself to envision another woman in the picture. At times, she launched into direct confrontation with Craig, accusing him of seeing another woman. But Craig always had an explanation when Becky confronted him on his mysterious and unexplained whereabouts—*his truck had broken down, he had to help a friend out of a jam, it was this, it was that.* The idea that Craig was a cross-dresser who was routinely on the town with others of the same persuasion never entered Becky's mind.

It was the size 14, sparkling gold spiked heels hidden under the seat of his pickup truck that eventually blew Craig's cover, and the confrontation that followed finally caused Craig to admit what he'd been doing. To this day, though, Becky is as confused about the reaction of some of her friends and acquaintances as she is about Craig's cross-dressing.

> *You know what just blows me away? I tell somebody what happened and they look at me like there's something weird about me—like there's nothing wrong with cross-dressing and I'm the one that's weird 'cause I can't accept it. I even talked to Craig's mother—right after I found out. You've got to understand. I was going nuts. Here's this guy I'm totally involved with. We're living together and I don't have a clue what's going on. Then I find out he's this cross-dresser. Yeah. You might say I went nuts. Well I found all this other stuff he had hidden at our house, and I went to see his mother. I start pulling out all this stuff I found. Bras, panties, the gold heels. You know what she says? I couldn't believe it. She says, 'Well, I knew Craig always had a thing for women's underwear, but I didn't realize it had gone this far.' I still can't believe it. Everybody thinks I'm the one who's off base.*

Becky's story illustrates a couple of points relative to Romantic Deception. First, it calls our attention back to the original definition I offered—the idea that misrepresentation of *significant facts* is at the heart of Romantic Deception. The issue is that cross-dressing was something significant to Becky. It may have been something that was just slightly to the other side of conventional to Craig and a lot of other people, but to Becky it was something significant. For Becky, the fact that Craig was silent about that aspect of his sexuality engendered a strong sense of betrayal—a sense of betrayal no less painful than if Craig had actually been married or if he had lied about a hundred other things. The story also illustrates how image and silence can combine to promote deception and keep it alive. Craig's macho image, along with his silence on the subject of his sexuality, served only one person in the partnership: Craig. As Becky eventually told me:

> It never occurs to you to just ask some guy if he's a cross-dresser. Who would think of that? You make a joke with a guy. You ask him if he's gay or something like that. So you don't follow up by asking if he's a cross-dresser? So it's your fault? Get real!

In case after case a singular message came out of the interviews. It wasn't the fact that a woman had one picture of a man in her mind, only to find out that her partner didn't measure up. It was something that went deeper. For the women who found themselves on the receiving end of one or more status lies, the sense of betrayal was rooted in the act of lying. Indeed, in story after story, woman after woman echoed the same phrase: *It wasn't what he lied about that got me upset. It was the fact that he had lied.*

Explanatory Lies

> The first few times he told me something like that I believed him. I knew he was this outdoors type, so the idea that he was going fishing or hunting with his buddies made sense. I didn't even think about it. After we started having problems, though, I got a little suspicious, so finally I decided to go by his house on one of those weekends he was supposed to

*be out camping with his friends. There was this
strange car in the driveway. I got a cop friend of
mine to check out the license plate number. Turns
out the car belonged to a woman—this woman he
worked with. Now she's living with him.*

Gretchen, age 41

Explanatory lies come in all shapes and sizes, and they're used in
any number of circumstances. They may have to do with the
past, present, or future, and they can be told for a variety of reasons. For you, the benefit of knowing a little bit about the use of
explanatory lies can be significant. Though they may strike you
as insignificant lies in and of themselves, they often point to a
much larger picture of deception.

Filling in the Blanks and Connecting Markers

Marker is a term that refers to a specific bit of information
your partner transmits to you in the course of a conversation.
It could be a specific reference to where he grew up, how many
brothers and sisters he has, what he does for a living, or where
he works. Markers are instrumental in defining who a person
is (or claims to be), and if you're like most people, you rely
heavily on the markers your partner utters to make your decisions about whether or not you want the relationship to move
forward.

Certainly, one of the characteristics of a big-time liar
(whether he's lying in the context of an intimate relationship
or some other set of circumstances) is that one lie has a way of
generating another lie. The result is that big-time liars end up
telling a bundle of lies—creating something akin to a house of
cards. This pattern of telling a bundle of lies is particularly
characteristic of Romantic Liars and no doubt partly linked to
the amount of communication that is required in an intimate
relationship.

It's one thing if an anonymous con artist targets you for deception. His aim is usually to establish your trust for a transitory period—long enough to gain your confidence, but not so long as to leave himself open to the threat of exposure. The traditional con artist may rely on a few strategic lies to establish that level of trust, but his eyes are usually set on a goal with a short-term pay-off strategy.

For example, what he might have planned is a bank account or credit card swindle of your assets, or a worthless home repair contract that will have you forking over cash for work that's never done. To pull it off, he'll need a few lies to establish his credibility, but they'll be crafted for delivery in an immediate and specific set of circumstances.

An intimate relationship, however, is very different. The communication is usually very long-running, so much so that a Romantic Liar faces the need to use explanatory lies at any number of points along the way. A lie might be successfully told at one point in the relationship, but often that same lie has to be backed up with yet another lie at a later time down the road, particularly if you start asking questions.

For example, a man who tells you some fantastic tales about his heroic military service might be able to get away with those tales for quite a while, particularly if his tales are set in the jungles of Vietnam or the desert lands of Kuwait. If you're like most people, you're unlikely to have a built-in storehouse of knowledge about those places. As a result, you're probably not in a position to determine on the spot that you're being told a whopper. If, however, you start asking some questions about where he was when he went into the military, where he spent his months in training, and how long he served, he's suddenly transported into a situation where answers are required. All of a sudden, you've put him in the position of having to fill in the blanks on his resume. Now he's having to tell you some more lies. He can ill afford to tell you he can't remember.

If his claim is that he got a divorce three years ago and you start boxing him into a corner with questions about where he was living at that time, you might also ask what he was doing in the way of work back them. If that's something he's failed to mention in the past, he'll have to once again fill in the blanks and connect the markers—explaining time segments on his resume and maybe even trying to make sense of the connection between a job back then and the job he has now.

Practiced liars won't have much difficulty coming up with the information that's necessary to fill in the blanks or connect the markers, because they don't have to rely on the truth. They can and will say whatever is necessary to provide an explanation. So what does all that mean for you? Does it mean the deception simply continues and you remain totally in the dark? Not necessarily. In fact, when an explanatory lie is told, it can ultimately prove to be very revealing, provided you know how to process it. Remember: Romantic Liars generally tell a bundle of lies. Like potato chips, there's no such thing as just one. Every time you box a Romantic Liar into a corner by forcing him to give you answers, there's always a chance that one or more of his answers will be something you could eventually check out. There's always a chance that he provides you with some information that eventually proves to be false.

If I were to offer you one rule of thumb when it comes to catching a Romantic Liar, it would be this: Don't try to catch him in the act of lying; instead, focus your efforts on catching him after the fact. I would also offer a second rule of thumb in that regard: When you're dealing with a Romantic Liar, it's often a good practice to ask some questions, sit back, and let the lies surface. Better yet (and assuming you find out a few facts about your partner in advance and without his knowledge), try to ask a few questions that you already know the answer to.

Let's say, for example, that you've been dating someone for a few weeks and you go to his house for dinner. Maybe a few weeks later you're over at his house again and you ask him when he bought his house. His answer could be very revealing, particularly if you've already been to the courthouse and you're determined that he's not the person who owns it. If he responds by telling you that he doesn't own the house—he's renting the place or house-sitting for a friend who relocated—that's fine. On the other hand, you've got a problem on your hands if he tells you he bought it two years ago. That one little lie becomes a very important clue in the overall scheme of things. The issue isn't whether or not he has the resources to own a home of his own; the issue is the lying in response to a direct question.

Any Form, Any Fashion

By now you're probably getting the picture. There's really no limit when, where, how, or why an explanatory lie might be told in the course of a relationship. It's simply the sort of lie a Romantic Liar is apt to reach for when he's forced to explain anything. It might be the past that has to be explained or it might be the future. It may be a lie that covers several years or just a few hours. Consider the possibilities:

Long-term Explanatory Lies

Depending on how he's constructed the picture he's painted for you, a Romantic Liar might find himself in the position of having to explain what he was doing those few years between when he graduated from college and the present day. Maybe he's told you where he went to school and when he finished, but what if that was four years ago and he's telling you he just moved to town? Where was he in the intervening years and what was he doing?

If he's really a truth teller, he'll have some specific answers and they'll make sense. What's more, there will probably be some information in those answers that will be verifiable in one way or another. On the other hand, if he's been lying, and particularly if he's got something he wants to hide, the story about the intervening years may be chock full of falsehoods. Yes, the story might make sense. But that doesn't mean it's true. And that's the point to remember. A truthful explanation is one thing; an explanatory lie is another. If what he's told you yields information that doesn't check out, it's a strong sign that there's some serious deception underway.

Short-term Explanatory Lies

Depending on how frequently you and your partner are actually in the presence of one another, a Romantic Liar may need to tell more than a few short-term explanatory lies. These are the lies he would tell if he needs to explain his whereabouts and activities for a few hours earlier in the day or a few hours last night. The problem with short-term explanatory lies is that they aren't all that easy to check out.

A long-term lie might give you some specific bits of factual information that you could eventually verify, but a short-term lie usually puts you in the position of looking a little bit like the inquisitor from hell when your doubts or suspicions come to the surface. For example, if a man tells you he's got to cancel your plans for the evening because a business engagement was unexpectedly firmed up, there's probably little you could do to realistically verify that what he's telling you is the truth. The same thing applies if your partner tells you he was out with the guys last night when you were trying repeatedly to reach him. When it comes to short-term explanatory lies, about the only thing that would tip you off to some underlying deception would be that the explanations (in this case, those repeated *night out with the boys*) start to have a familiar ring to them.

Past Versus the Future

Romantic Liars don't limit their explanatory lying to the past. Sometimes it's the future that has to be explained away in advance. If, for example, you're involved with someone who has you thinking you're his one and only, it pays to beware of business meetings, hunting trips, or other out-of-town sojourns that are announced well in advance. Preannounced absences can certainly be legitimate, but they often are the red flag that signals your partner is involved with another woman.

For example, there are the men you'll read about in a later section (war heroes, secret agents, and other nutballs) who make use of a very handy future-oriented lie. These are the would-be James Bond characters who tell their targets that they're being called away *on assignment.*

One of the more novel future-oriented explanatory lies I heard about was a fellow's claim that he had been called to jury duty and that he expected to be tied up for several days. It turned out that the jury duty story was just a cover for the fact that her partner's in-laws were coming to town (something he wanted to keep secret since he was pretending he was single). The jury duty story, complete with references to how he was going to have to make up his lost time at work by working at night, gave him the perfect story to cover the time he would be spending with his wife's parents.

Road Map Resources

Because there are a constellation of explanatory lies that usually creep into a deceptive relationship, partners on the receiving end often find themselves awash in a sea of suspicions. Any one explanatory lie by itself doesn't necessarily result in a specific suspicion rising to the surface, but because explanatory lies have a way of growing into a bundle of falsehoods, they are very likely to eventually raise the red flag when they're taken together. The lessons in all this? There are at least a couple that come to mind.

First, always remember how you came to know (or think you know) your partner in the first place. If he's given you specific information while he's filling in the resume gaps in response to a direct question you've asked him, it might do you some good to remind yourself that it was information you had to ask for. To be fair, he might have eventually gotten around to giving you the very same information, but who's to say? What's more, the information you glean as a result of some direct questioning on your part might be the very sort of information that you would want to verify. In particular you might want to take some steps to verify any information that covers a significant chunk of your partner's resume. In short, the information could turn out to be part of your road map to uncovering deceit.

The second lesson has to do with how explanatory lies are often hatched. It's safe to say that most explanatory lies you're apt to encounter will be the ones that are born of the moment and crafted by a Romantic Liar to meet everyday but changing circumstances. For example, you've asked your partner if you can meet him at his office so the two of you can have lunch, but he doesn't really work where he says he works. Maybe you've asked to have dinner at his place, for a change, but that won't do because he's got a wife and three kids living with him. Maybe you've asked him where he was until all hours of the night when you were trying to reach him by telephone. All of those are situations that might call for an explanatory lie.

Human behavior being what it is, there's a certain amount of predictability to it. If a Romantic Liar uses an explanatory lie (something along the lines of *I was out with the boys 'til all hours*), and he concludes the lie has worked, he's apt to rely on it again sometime in the future. By the same token, if a business trip scenario works once, it's likely it will work again, or so he's apt to reason. The result of all this is that explanatory lies can take on a discernible pattern. And that's what you should be looking for. If you sense a pattern emerging, you should regard it as a potential red flag. Even if you can't verify some or any of the explanations he's handing you, it's time to double back around and start verifying some of the factual bits of information he's revealed in times past. Once again, those patterned sorts of explanation can turn out to be your road map.

Personal Tragedy Lies

The holiday season was approaching, and Mindy was determined that it would be a joyous one. She and Tony had been dating for about three months, and all the signs were telling her it was a serious relationship. Tony was with her almost every night, and it was hard to imagine that he could have been more devoted.

When Mindy started talking about Christmas, though, Tony's demeanor changed noticeably. What really shocked her was Tony's announcement that he no longer celebrated Christmas. Mindy didn't really know how to react, but that was probably a good thing, given what Tony told her next. According to poor Tony, his parents had been killed in a head-on traffic accident three years ago—on Christmas Eve, no less.

Mindy was convinced that she would still be able to make it a nice holiday; it would just be a matter of celebrating in a low-key sort of way. By the time the holidays came and went, though, Mindy was glad she hadn't gone too overboard with presents for Tony.

The devoted suitor managed to totally disappear from the scene. Mindy later learned that Tony had a complete family right across town—one wife, two kids. She also found out that Tony's parents were very alive and living in New Mexico. Mindy's best guess is that the lie about how they were killed on Christmas Eve was all part of a way to cover for the fact that he wouldn't be around during the holidays.

Tony's lie is a classic example of what I call the *personal tragedy lie*. When we enter this realm of Romantic Deception, we begin to see just how far outside social convention a Romantic Liar can travel. It's one thing for someone to brazenly portray himself as having earned a string of advanced degrees when he actually dropped out of college, but it's quite another for him to claim his parents are dead when they're still very much alive. Claims that family members are deceased or critically ill represent some of the more common personal tragedy lies, but Romantic Liars also frequently talk about dear friends, coworkers, ex-girlfriends, or former fiancées who met untimely deaths.

Personal tragedy lies have a way of catching you off guard. They speak to loss, grief, sorrow, and personal wounding. They can pull at your heartstrings and cause you to be thankful for the very life you're leading, even if it's less than what you'd always hoped for. A personal tragedy lie can involve the Romantic Liar, himself, but typically it involves at least one other person (for example, a fiancée who committed suicide, despite the Romantic Liar's heroic efforts to save her). Death and disease seem to form the foundation for most personal tragedy lies, but personal hardships, traumatic events, or the loss of personal fortunes can also serve as prominent themes.

Personal tragedy lies may or may not be told with elaborate detail, and they're likely to surface at any stage of relationship. The mere telling of the lie is usually enough to get the target totally off balance. Consider how you might respond if the man you were involved with told you his daughter has leukemia, his wife died of cancer, or his best friend died right beside him during one of the last battles of the war in Vietnam.

What would your reaction be? Would you feel some sympathy—maybe even a little empathy? OK; let me ask it another way. Assume someone's sitting across the table from you and he tells you one of those personal tragedy stories—maybe the one about his ex-girlfriend committing suicide. Do you think you might just roll your eyes, adopt a sarcastic tone, and say "Sure she did; and I'm a Nobel Prize winner?" Even if you're fairly cynical, it's difficult to imagine that you'd react that way.

And that's the whole point. The *content* of a personal tragedy lie is usually enough to call forth an almost automatic response of sympathy. We're simply socialized that way. It's no wonder, then, that personal tragedy lies have a high believability component. You may later discover that the lies were total fabrications, but initially you're likely to take them as the truth. *Who would lie about such a thing?* you're very apt to ask yourself (if you ask yourself any questions at all).

For a Romantic Liar to successfully deliver a personal tragedy lie, the most important requirement is that he has the nerve to tell the lie in the first place. It also helps if the liar can muster up some teary eyes and a little quiver in his voice when he tells his tale of woe. Lest you think that's not possible, take my word for it. In all the cases where a personal tragedy lie had been told, the victim was always quick to mention how genuine the Romantic Liar was in his telling of the lie.

It's anyone's guess as to why Romantic Liars make use of personal tragedy lies. One obvious reason, of course, is that they're looking for a little sympathy. Equally likely, however, is the notion that a personal tragedy lie, if used properly, can effectively remove an instrumental party from the playing field. Many a married man, for example, has explained away the existence of a wife by claiming she is dead. Darlene's story about Rich's dead wife is a good case in point. It also has a slightly humorous twist in the sense that some of Darlene's pals eventually got even with Rich.

⁂

Darlene met Rich while she was working on a consulting assignment in Atlanta. When Rich explained that he, too, was in Atlanta on a temporary basis, his living arrangements made sense. He frequently had to return to his hometown halfway across the state because his seven-year-old daughter was living with his parents. That's the way it had been since his wife died as a result of cancer three years ago.

Rich's efforts to give his daughter the right environment in the face of such tragedy immediately struck a chord with Darlene. After all, Darlene, who was recently divorced, was facing much the same situation. Her career frequently took her out of town and away from her five-year-old daughter, Jenny. Like Rich's family, though, Darlene's parents had stepped in to bring some sense of security to Jenny's young life.

Like so many other cases of Romantic Deception, the underlying deceit eventually came to light only by accident. In the case of Rich's deception of Darlene, it was a seemingly inconsequential remark that Darlene made to Jake, one of Rich's buddies. When Darlene said something about *three years ago when Rich's wife died*, Jake's face suddenly took on a bewildered expression. *Wife died? Rich's wife isn't dead!* Jake said. And that's when all hell broke loose.

In the end, Darlene was able to extract her pound of flesh, if only indirectly. As it turned out, most of Rich's friends really liked Darlene. Indeed, some of them were incensed enough at what Rich had done that they waged a month-long campaign of sending Rich sympathy cards and black wreaths to his office just to remind him of his deceased wife.

Even with her knowledge of how some of Rich's own friends stepped up to the plate to teach him a lesson, Darlene still harbors some feelings of bitterness. Listen to her words:

> *I got over him pretty quick. I was totally pissed off when it happened, but I got over him. My daughter, though, that's another story. When I was dating Rich he spent a lot of time with her. Whenever she came to see me on a weekend, he went out of his way to do stuff with her. She got real close to him, and then it ended. It took her a real long time to get over that. When a kid is five years old there's only so much you can tell her. And I'll tell you what else. It still kind of burns me that he had all his friends thinking I knew he was married. See—that's how he pulled it off with them. He just let them think it didn't make any difference to me that he was married. At the same time, he's telling me his wife is dead. Thank goodness those guys turned out to be my friends. Rich didn't care what they thought of me.*

As with so many other facets of a Romantic Liar's behavior, it's very easy to get all caught up in wanting to know why he does what he does, but my response to that sort of thinking has always been pretty straightforward. Don't waste your time.

Whether you want to know why he tells a particular type of lie or why he lies in general, it's just a waste of your time. Just knowing you've got a liar on your hands should be enough to give you the warning you need.

Obviously, anybody's life can be punctuated with real tragedy at any time, so it would be unfair to give a wholesale dismissal to any tale of tragedy that might come out of your partner's mouth. On the other hand, forewarned is forearmed. If you ever find yourself listening to a tale that could reasonably fit into the personal tragedy lie category, take the time to ask yourself one simple question: *How do you know that what he's telling you is true?* It sounds a little callous—maybe even a little cruel—so I can understand if you find the idea a little bit abhorrent. On the other hand, I've seen enough evidence to indicate that personal tragedy lies are really quite common in the world of Romantic Deception. And that's reason enough to let your mind do some wandering and wondering.

Just Plain Crazy Lies: War Heroes, Secret Agents, and Other Nutballs

The men who take Romantic Deception to the limit belong in this category, and the lies they tell ultimately make us wonder just how unstable some Romantic Liars might be. These are the men who, some would say, appear to be living in a fantasy world. Common examples include men who present themselves as decorated war heroes or members of the intelligence community. Other examples would include men such as Taylor, the fake physician you read about earlier. Just to give you an idea of how far he was willing to go to foster a false illusion and keep the charade going, Taylor used all sorts of props to punctuate the picture. He had a habit of showing up at Allison's apartment wearing a freshly starched lab coat, complete with his hospital identification badge clipped to the chest pocket. He often had a stethoscope curled up and noticeably tucked in a side pocket, along with a pager he routinely used to check in with the physician's answering service. The phony British accent never left him. As I said earlier, he could come out of a dead sleep speaking in a British accent—despite the fact that he was from Iowa.

There's no doubt about it; the Romantic Liars who fall into this category are perhaps the most interesting and curious of the lot. Because the lies they tend to tell generally strike us as wholly exaggerated, these are the men who cause us to pause and shake our heads in bewilderment. Because their lies are so extraordinary, liars in this category are wonderful subjects for any study of Romantic Deception. If nothing else, the men in this more extreme category give us clues to what Romantic Deception is all about in its purest form. Just take a look at some of these rather curious characters.

⁂

I was interviewing Patsy, a real-estate broker in her early forties, about her relationship with Jeff. She was listing each and every lie Jeff told—at least all that she could remember—when I interrupted her somewhere between Lie #10 and Lie #11. My experience with other tales of deception told me that Jeff was a likely candidate for the just-plain-crazy category. Based on what I had learned about other Romantic Liars in that category, I asked Patsy if Jeff ever claimed affiliation with the intelligence service.

Patsy was a little surprised by my question. *That's really interesting,* she said. *As a matter of fact, he sort of did.* Then she went on to relate this story.

Jeff had told Patsy he served in an intelligence unit in Vietnam with a particular U.S. senator, and a particularly prominent U.S. senator, at that. I remarked to Patsy that my instincts were telling me Jeff was lying about that. I also told Patsy I would do a little biographical research on the senator in question and that I would get back to her, adding that I really didn't think the senator in question had ever served in Vietnam.

As it turned out, I was right, and I reported the information back to Patsy. Now here's the interesting part. She later confronted Jeff with that information, telling him that his Vietnam story was one more of his misrepresentations (based on what I had found out), but Jeff simply came back with another lie. He said he wasn't talking about a *U.S.* senator. He said he was talking about a *state senator* of the same name who had served in the legislature in a neighboring state. As you might expect, it turned out that nobody by that name had ever served in the legislature of that neighboring state.

What Patsy experienced is telling in two ways. First, Jeff was running around claiming he served in an intelligence unit in Vietnam, and, as an added attraction, he wanted people to believe he was right there at the side of a man who would one day be a major political figure. The fact that Jeff threw in an added embellishment about being a pal of a national political figure is the sort of thing that warrants his entry into the nutball category. Equally telling is the way Jeff reacted when Patsy confronted him. He simply modified his lie and didn't miss a beat. Getting caught in a big-time lie apparently didn't phase Jeff in the least.

In another case, Darcey found herself involved with Paul, an attractive man in his late forties, who claimed to be a retired Air Force officer. But Paul wasn't just any retired officer. He claimed he *still occasionally did some work for the State Department*. Here are a few of the details.

At first, the story seemed to make sense, or so Darcey thought. Paul had taken her to a number of retired officers' association functions and everything pointed to his being a well-liked and regular sort of guy. As their relationship developed, Paul would occasionally make other references to his continued part-time work for the State Department, but he was also always very quick to add that he'd *already said too much*.

Not too long into the relationship, Paul had to leave town every few weeks, ostensibly for his mysterious assignments. Paul usually got his orders for his special assignments via phone calls from his contacts in Washington, or so he said. In fact, Darcey was at Paul's home one night when one of those curious telephone calls came. Darcey only got bits and pieces of one side of the conversation, so she could hardly be expected to understand all that was going on. Besides that, it was Darcey's first experience with anyone living a life of espionage, intrigue, or whatever it was, so she didn't ask too many questions.

Over time, the trips out of town became more numerous, but Paul had a habit of always documenting that indeed he'd been somewhere out of the country. A simple or small gesture, perhaps, but Paul would always return with some coins or currency from a foreign country in his pocket—a little something to add credibility to his stories.

To say that Paul eventually got very weird would be an understatement. On more than one occasion he lapsed into what Darcey described as an extreme melancholic state. Whenever that happened, he would sob and carry on in a totally self-deprecating way about all the horrible things he'd done in war and all the horrible things he was still doing on behalf of his government. *Oh that his life could change and he could be free of the dirty business of espionage!*

As it turned out, Darcey eventually determined that Paul was still in the good old U.S.A. all those times he said he was on assignment overseas. He was also spending some serious time with other women. Darcey's not certain where Paul got the newly minted coins and currency from all those foreign countries, but her best bet is that he simply popped into the local coin dealer's store a few blocks from his house.

You might think that the number of cases falling into the category of war heroes, secret agents, and other nutballs would be small, but the list of examples could go on and on. If the interviews I conducted are any indication, there are a lot of nutballs running around out there.

Some Romantic Liars claim a direct connection with the intelligence community, such as, the men who say they're actively working for the C.I.A., State Department, Defense Intelligence Agency, and so forth. Others, like Paul, present themselves as having a more indirect affiliation—men who claim they *still take on some assignments every now and then.* It's not uncommon for men in this category of would-be spies and secret agents to let their tall tales include claims of being on assassination teams that have operated all over the world in the interest of our national security. It's little wonder that victims of Romantic Liars in this category often grow fearful of their partners.

Some Romantic Liars pass up the chance to be a spy or secret agent, remaining content to pretend they're working in more routine law enforcement circles. For example, Darrel, who was actually an apprentice electrician, presented himself as a highly paid, always in demand, security consultant who specialized in contract work for the F.B.I.

Another example was Clint, who claimed he worked for a federal strike force that targeted organized crime, even though his father was connected to the Mafia (or so he said). Ashley, his latest in what turned out to be a string of girlfriends who were fed the same line, eventually found out that Clint was pretty much living off credit cards and a generous father. With the help of a private investigator, she learned that Clint had told her a string of whoppers. He had lied about everything from where he graduated from college (he never graduated from any college, let alone the school he said he attended) to his marital status (he was still married to the woman he married more than twenty years ago).

Some men avoid any reference to connections with intelligence or law enforcement circles, opting instead for a simple, but highly distinguished and sometimes heroic, military career. Among true veterans, they're known as "Wannabes"—men who want you to think they had significant military careers. Some of these characters have gone so far as to purchase all sorts of military awards, service medallions, and other emblematic phony evidence from an Army/Navy supply retail outlet.

One bona fide Vietnam veteran who remains active in veterans' organizations told me that "Wannabes" are actually quite common—far more numerous that most people would think. He also said it's highly unlikely you'll ever meet a "Wannabe" who claims he was a cook or a supply sergeant. On the contrary, heroic service is a central part of the theme when a "Wannabe" tells a war story. When you're dealing with a "Wannabe," what you'll likely hear are stories about how he was a P.O.W. or how he won the Congressional Medal of Honor.

As to what pushes a Romantic Liar to the level of deception we've been discussing here, we can only speculate. For all the reasons I mention throughout this book, the odds of really getting inside the head of a Romantic Liar are not strong. At best, we're left with hypothetical explanations and educated guesses.

In the case of men who pose as members of the law enforcement or intelligence community, I suspect their phony identities are largely invented for practical reasons. As long as a man can claim an occupation that, by definition, requires some secrecy, he's really quite free to be anywhere—anytime—and he does not have to answer any questions. In that sense, claims of involvement with law enforcement or intelligence circles provide Romantic Liars with all-purpose excuses that can serve them in any number of circumstances.

For example, a would-be James Bond who doesn't want you to know he's really married enjoys a significant benefit as a result of his mythical spy status. If you need his presence at a special function (an office holiday party or a class reunion, for example), but he's fearful he'll run into someone who knows that he's actually married, all he has to do is tell you he has to go out of town *on assignment*. A would-be James Bond who's really out of work doesn't have to tell you where he is during the day or how he's spending his time. After all (assuming you buy his story about being in the intelligence community), where he goes and what he does are things he *just can't talk about*.

While some of the phony identities these men dream up can be explained as practical efforts to fashion an *all-purpose excuse*, it still seems fair to question just how psychologically unstable the men in this category might be. In contrast to a run-of-the-mill Romantic Liar—someone who tells just a singular status lie or an availability lie or two, for example—the men who wear the label of just-plain-crazy liars are the ones who present an image that is almost totally false. They're the ones who typically present a bundle of lies—a package of lies that starts out with a phony occupation and goes from there. They present images that are constructed from top to bottom, and they lie about their past as well as their present. To say that they have some form of pathology would not be an understatement.

What All This Tells Us

When you begin to examine all the different lies Romantic Liars tell, it's very easy to get caught up in the details of the specific lies and, in the process, loose sight of the larger picture—namely, what all this tells us about the way some relationships are lived out. If we look beyond the details of the specific lies, it becomes apparent that there are a lot of Romantic Liars operating on the assumption that they'll never get caught. Even if they harbor a fear that one day the truth will be revealed, we have to assume that they think the gamble is worth it.

Of course, the obvious question is *What is the gamble all about?* What on earth would prompt a person to misrepresent, fabricate, lie, and deceive on the level we've been discussing? What on earth would cause someone to totally ignore the feelings of a significant other and engage in a charade of substantial proportion?

As I've said so many times before, we can only speculate as to what is really going on inside the mind of a Romantic Liar. Does he do it because he takes delight in duping people? Is it just a matter of social sport with him—an attempt to win the interest and attention of women he might not attract otherwise? Or does he adopt a phony identity or keep parts of his true identity secret because he has a horribly wounded self-image of some sort? Is it really a matter of some serious psychological problems that propel him into a life that sometimes reaches fantasy proportions?

Speculations along those lines are interesting in an academic sense, but they're really of no consequence in the reality of a relationship with a Romantic Liar. As a matter of fact, speculations like that can be downright dangerous, especially if you let them get the best of you. There is no better way to prolong the entanglement with a Romantic Liar than to discover the deception and then decide that you're the one who's going to bring it to a halt. There's no bigger fantasy than to think that you're the one who can cause him to change his behavior as soon as you find out what makes him tick.

Without any knowledge of what's really going on in his mind, the most we can do is consider the nature of their lies and how they tell them. And that takes us back to the point I raised earlier. One has to assume that most Romantic Liars (at least the ones I heard about) are operating on the assumption that they won't get caught, or with the thought that getting caught is of little consequence. And in the end, maybe that's the core defining characteristic of Romantic Liars. As my friend Angela remarked one day when we were talking about my research and the men who were the central characters, *maybe it's an arrogant form of insanity—or maybe it's an insane form of arrogance.* I'm not certain which it is, but I'm convinced Angela is on the right track.

SECTION III

The Six Signs

For reasons I alluded to in an earlier chapter, I'm not a strong proponent of theories that suggest you can spot a liar if you focus on things like facial expressions and body language. By the same token, I also don't believe that just anyone and everyone can develop the requisite skills to interrogate a partner to the point that he willingly confesses about any lies he's told you. Some people are probably gifted when it comes to deception detection through face-to-face observational and interrogation skills, but most people aren't. Besides that, those are skills that are hardly acquired overnight. Instead, I subscribe to the notion that the best way to catch a liar is to turn your attention to the overall patterns of interaction that are taking place in the relationship.

In this section we'll be looking at what I refer to as the six signs—subtle clues and indications that point to the presence of deception in a relationship. They're the red flags that can warn you something is very likely very wrong. The signs have to do with everything from how your partner behaves to the overall structure of your relationship. There are also some clues that go straight to the matter of how you react to what's going on around you.

The signs are simply *high probability* clues—signs that should alert you to the possibility of deception in your relationship. At present there's no such thing as a perfect set of predictors when it comes to a deceptive relationship, and I doubt there ever will be. On the other hand, the presence of one or more of the signs should cause you to pause long enough to maybe think about your relationship in a little different light. In virtually every case of deception I heard about, at least one of the signs was present. That's what leads me to believe they are valuable clues, indeed.

The First Sign: Information Control

> *Kirby and I were having all sorts of problems and things were going downhill. I was telling one of my friends about it and she started asking all of the questions about him. I guess that's when it really hit me—I really didn't know the first thing about him. It was really scary. Kirby knew my entire life story, but I didn't know the first thing about him. My friend sort of took me step by step—asking all of these questions. She's real savvy; I'm certain she knew what she was doing. She just wanted to let me know how much I didn't know.*
>
> **Kathleen, age 29**

A Romantic Liar's ability to control the information flow in a relationship is one of his greatest assets. When you meet a Romantic Liar, you can count on the fact that he'll always know more about you than you know about him. It all starts with his ability to direct the information traffic—how much of what kind of information is transmitted by whom to whom. Since he usually starts controlling information from the minute you first meet him, it's possible to uncover an early sign of deception, provided you know what you're looking for.

Be Aware of Information Shutdowns

> *He told me he really didn't date a lot because he*
> *was sort of shy. I remember how that made me*
> *feel. See, I am a real talker by nature, and I usu-*
> *ally don't hold back. But I liked Allen right off the*
> *bat. I remember telling myself that I ought to go*
> *easy on him and not get him all unnerved with a*
> *lot of questions.*

Terri, age 39

One of the first things to look for is the possibility that your partner's getting away with *information shutdown*. It's anyone's guess whether Allen's story was intentional or not, but the effect of what he said about being shy temporarily suspended some of the normal flow of information. And that's what information shutdown is all about. Information shutdown occurs whenever there's something your partner can't talk about for whatever reason—he's too shy, some experience in the past was too painful, he doesn't feel comfortable, and so on. If a Romantic Liar deliberately uses information shutdown as an interaction strategy, it's almost guaranteed you'll be kept in the dark for quite a while. You might eventually figure out what's going on, but it could take weeks or months. Information shutdown forces you into a defensive position. If you're going to get any information from your partner, you'll have to drag it out of him.

Some Romantic Liars give the impression that they're the shy, quiet type. All it takes is the right statement, delivered in just the right way at the front end of a relationship, to set the tone for what happens later. It may be that your partner really is the shy, quiet type, but who's to say? In Terri's case, for example, all it took was one seemingly innocent remark by Allen, and she decided to go easy on him.

In the case of Bridgett, it was Ben's story about *a wonderful gal who broke the engagement because her family thought that he didn't measure up.* Like Terri, Bridgett held back, thinking Ben would reveal himself in due time.

*You know he told me that story on our first date—
how his fiancée broke off the engagement 'cause
her parents didn't think he was good enough. He
made it seem like they thought he didn't go to the
right school or he didn't have the right job, or there
was something wrong with this family. I guess it
really had an effect on me.*

*I had this picture in my mind of her parents
putting him through the grinder. I was thinking to
myself how horrible that must have been. For all I
know, he was never engaged in the first place. That
was probably another one of his lies. But I know I
believed it at the time. I wasn't about to start asking him a whole bunch of questions. I thought I
was being kind: I was just being stupid.*

Terri and Bridgett were maneuvered into defensive postures in
different ways, but they shared one thing in common. Both were
taken in by seemingly inconsequential statements—comments that
seemed to have little significance at the time, but remarks that
turned out to be strategically important.

Anytime you make the mistake of assuming a defensive posture
in the process of information exchange—anytime you hold back on
your questions of a new partner—you put yourself at risk for two reasons. First, you necessarily limit the amount of information you're
actually going to get out of someone. The longer it takes to learn who
and what you're dealing with, the greater you risk potential harm.
Second, your willingness to assume a defensive posture in the process
of information exchange gives your partner a silent signal that says a
lot about your *personal boundaries*. It says a lot about what you'll tolerate. When someone deliberately uses the tactic of information shutdown and you go along with it, there's only one way to interpret it.
You're willing to move forward in a relationship, even though you
don't have a lot of knowledge about your partner. Chances are your
partner will take note, particularly if he's trying to deceive you.

A word to the wise at this point: Always be alert to how much information your partner is sharing with you from the first meeting forward. It can be one of *your* best clues to what the real agenda is all about. It is also very likely *his* first clue about how far he can go in his deception with you.

Be Aware of Information Balance

A lot of Romantic Liars stop short of total information shutdown, but they still manage to keep the amount of information significantly out of balance. As I've said before, a Romantic Liar will always know more about you than you know about him. Here's how Angie described what it was like when she was getting to know Doug.

> I used to be all hung up on this conversation thing—I liked guys who could carry on a good conversation. Well, Doug was good at carrying on a conversation all right. I guess you could call him a pro. He had me doing all the talking.
>
> It was maybe a week after I found out he was married that I realized how in the dark I was. Doug knew everything about me—everything from where I was born to the name of my dog. I knew he was a sports nut and he liked to drink beer. Oh yeah. He also liked country and western music. That's all I really knew.

Be Aware of Information Tone

To understand the meaning of information tone, consider how Danielle described her initial encounters with Clark, a man who successfully managed to hide the fact that he was unemployed during the three months they were dating. Their pattern of communication was established the first time they met.

> *The thing that attracted me to Clark was the way*
> *he just talked and talked and seemed so easygoing.*
> *Sometimes I have a hard time meeting people, so I*
> *really liked that about him. I guess it made me feel*
> *real comfortable. Now I think back on it and I*
> *know Clark never said anything that was real*
> *important—you know—he didn't talk about his*
> *family, or where he grew up, or where he thought*
> *he was going with his career. Now I know why. For*
> *starters, he didn't have a job.*

Clark's behavior is typical of a lot of Romantic Liars. He was able to fill the air with a nonstop stream of conversation, but he never said anything of substance. He would talk endlessly about insignificant matters, but when it came to anything that got close to revealing anything about his background, he was noticeably silent.

In a slight variation on the same theme, Brian was able to pepper his conversations with all sorts of details. In fact, it was largely the detail in all his stories that seemed to give Brian a measure of credibility in Susan's eyes.

> *If we were just talking on the phone, he'd give me all*
> *this detail about how he spent his day. I mean he*
> *talked about meetings he had to go to and problems*
> *he had to deal with. He'd talk about piles of paper*
> *on his desk and who was asking him to do what. You*
> *know—when we were talking about things like*
> *that—he would rattle off all these details. For all I*
> *know, he was telling the truth when we were talking*
> *over the phone—you know—about his job and so*
> *forth. Maybe that was part of the deal, I don't know.*
>
> *I just know that a lot of what he told me seemed very*
> *believable just because there was so much detail in*
> *it. But later on when I started getting suspicious, I*
> *realized I didn't have much to go on. When it came*

to who he really was and his background and stuff like that, there was a big zero. The details weren't there. He had told me he graduated from the University of Colorado, but that was about it. Later—after I started getting suspicious—I checked on that. He'd never even been at the University of Colorado.

There's a lesson in commentaries like those, and it's this: There's a big difference between *information quantity* and *information quality*. If you think you and your partner have good communication, that's wonderful. But it always pays to take a hard look at what you're communicating about. If the conversation is there, but it's essentially hollow and it doesn't go to the heart of who your partner really is, it's not really communication. As a rule, conversation without communication is a warning signal.

Be Aware of Information Context

Some Romantic Liars are successful because they operate in narrowly defined environments and settings shielded from the outside world. A Romantic Liar may escort you all over town and fill your calendar with dinners at all the finest places, but that doesn't mean he's operating out in the open.

To operate out in the open means he's with you in the company of others—your family, friends, and coworkers or his family, friends, and coworkers. When the only significant information you have about your partner is information you gleaned in semiprivate circumstances, you need to be on guard. Listen to these voices of experience.

Now I know why he never introduced me to any of his friends. It makes sense. All of them knew he was married. He was living in a real small town and they had to know he was married. No wonder we never spent any time there. No wonder he

always came to see me. He always said there was
nothing to do where he lived. Yeah. Right. Nothing
to do but meet the wife and kids.

Cheryl, age 31

One of my friends at work met Jack and she told me
there was something strange about him—something
that didn't add up. I guess her intuition worked bet-
ter than mine. She told me she smelled a rat the
minute she met him. I wish now that we'd spent
more time around her and some of my other friends.
Maybe I would have figured it out earlier.

Jodi, age 27

Observations like that demonstrate why it's important to pay attention to *information context*. What your partner tells you about himself in the context of private conversations should always be regarded as just that—information he's passing along in a *nonpublic context*. What you're really looking for—at least if you really want to know who and what your partner is—are the bits and pieces of significant information he's willing to present in a public setting.

If he really graduated with an M.B.A. from Harvard, give him a chance to make that known in front of your friends and family. If he's given to telling war stories, let him have the opportunity to tell the same tales in front of other people, particularly some bona fide veterans. Maybe everything he says will withstand their scrutiny, but then again, maybe it won't. You'll never know unless you make an effort to find out.

The Second Sign: Impression Management

Like information control, impression management is something that starts at the beginning and continues throughout the life of a deceptive relationship. If Romantic Liars have a first principle that guides most of their behavior, I suggest it would be this: Creating an impression is one thing; backing it up is another matter altogether.

All of us are accustomed to a certain amount of impression management, even in the most routine of circumstances. All of us know a little bit about how the game is played. We know what's required in the way of impression management when we're out there interviewing for a job, just as we have some idea of what's required if we're going to impress someone on a first date. What separates a Romantic Liar from the rest of the pack, though, is the extent to which he'll go to manage an impression. For some Romantic Liars, there are no limits. Truly inventive Romantic Liars can make use of any number of mechanisms to give credibility to the impression they want to make.

Earlier I introduced you to the concept of a *marker*—a strategic piece of information that is dropped into a conversation. Markers are *strategic* in the sense that they help you define the person you're interacting with—strategic because they're often the elements you key in on when you're initially getting to know somebody.

By now it should be clear that part of a Romantic Liar's skill in fostering an illusion comes from his ability to string together the right markers in the right situations. Markers can come in response to a direct question from you or they can be dropped into a conversation in a seemingly spontaneous fashion. Somebody tells you where he grew up or where he went to school—those are markers. Somebody tells you where he lives or what he does for a living—those are markers.

The important thing about the use of a marker, of course, is that most of us assume that markers are honest statements. In the world of relationships, it's common for markers to stand as valid unless they're questioned or contradicted. Indeed, I dare say that most people enter into relationships with an assumption that any markers they paid attention to were actually statements of fact. No doubt a Romantic Liar knows that. What's more, he no doubt knows that most people don't take the time to verify the markers. It all goes back to what I said earlier about the *truth bias* that governs so much of our interaction with other people.

If you made it a practice to key in on markers and then you took the time to verify them, you might be very surprised at what you'd find out. If you're dealing with a Romantic Liar, I can almost guarantee you'd be surprised. And therein lies the lesson. If you want a clue to Romantic Deception, start with the markers. Remember: The markers foster the impression. It's just that simple. If for some reason you discover you don't have any markers to go on, that should tell you something right there. In the appendix to this book, you'll find a mountain of information that will help you if you want to check out what your partner's represented to you by the way of markers. The information is there; the choice is yours.

Props, Setting, and Friends

Depending on the nature and extent of the impression he's trying to foster, a Romantic Liar may rely on props, settings, and even a friend or two in any number of combinations to keep the deception going. In the case of Taylor, the phony medical doctor you read about earlier, props were almost central to the illusion he was trying to create. Taylor had all of them—lab coats with his name embroidered on them, a hospital identification badge, a beeper, and even a stethoscope.

It's hard to imagine that anyone would go to such lengths, but that's exactly what some Romantic Liars do. Some phony war heroes even have collections of combat ribbons and service awards, and some of the fake intelligence agents like to carry phony identification cards and locked briefcases with them wherever they go.

Some Romantic Liars don't operate alone. Instead, they call on friends to assist in the deception. You have to wonder why a bystander would be willing to get involved in such an insidious game as Romantic Deception, but don't spend too much time wondering. Just accept the fact; it happens quite frequently. For example, I've come across any number of cases in which friends have loaned a Romantic Liar everything from cars to clothes to houses, just to help him keep the game going for a little longer. In one case, for example, it was a willing friend who provided a phony setting. The phony setting, in turn, was central to the deception.

Larry, for example, greeted the guard at the gatehouse like they were best buddies each and every time he squired Tami to his swank home. Tami was operating on the assumption that Larry was the successful insurance executive he claimed he was. She didn't have any reason to doubt him. Plus, all the signs were right in front of her—a lovely home, a gated community, a pool in the backyard. What else did she need to know?

As it turned out there was a lot that Tami needed to know. When the truth finally came to light, it was almost more than Tami could comprehend. Larry didn't own the home at all. As a matter of fact, the home belonged to Larry's good buddy Dan. Since Dan was working overseas, Larry had the run of the place. It's a good thing he did, since Larry couldn't afford to be at his real house when he wanted to carry on with Tami. The situation over there was a little too crowded—what with Larry's wife and two kids.

⚜

The lesson in all this? Impressions can be valid and backed up by reality, but they can also be constructed out of thin air. To untangle the impression you have of someone—to begin to look at someone in an objective fashion—it's best to start with the markers. If the markers are valid, you're probably operating on the basis of an accurate impression. Discover that one of the markers is false, however, and you might be very surprised at what the bigger picture is all about.

The Third Sign: Tending Behaviors and Narrowing Tactics

If nothing else, the material you've read so far should convince you of a very important thing about Romantic Liars: They're tough to catch in the middle of a lie, at least in the beginning of the relationship. As your relationship goes on you might be able to do that, but remember—the goal is to sniff out a Romantic Liar before the game goes too far. Something you can do is to look for the *action clues* to deceit. The *action clues* are the outward signs that can signal a Romantic Liar at work—outward signs that have nothing to do with the content of any lies he's been telling.

Why Action Clues Surface

A Romantic Liar is usually trying to hide something important—the fact that he's married, the fact that he didn't go to school where he said he did, the fact that he isn't really working where he says he works, and so forth. As a result, he's not going to conduct his life the way a normal man would. Simply as a practical matter, big-time lying creates a situation for a Romantic Liar that's difficult to manage.

For example, a married man having an affair lives under a constant fear he'll be found out because his wife and girlfriend might have some mutual acquaintance or they could have a chance encounter that ultimately reveals the truth. A single man who's lied about his background always run the risk of public exposure if you have an unexpected meeting with someone who knows the truth. If a Romantic Liar's going to be successful, he has to constantly guard against the emergence of *contradictory knowledge*—any knowledge from *any* source that contradicts what he's represented to you as fact.

A skilled Romantic Liar might be able to control the flow of information coming out of his mouth, but he can't always control what comes out of the mouths of other people. And therein lies the reason behind the action clues to Romantic Deception. Assuming that a Romantic Liar has placed a high priority on keeping the deception alive, he'll more than likely work overtime to influence what kind of information might come your way. As a rule, eventually he'll rely on two categories of actions to keep you in the dark—*tending behaviors* and *narrowing tactics*.

Tending Behaviors

Tending behaviors are the things a Romantic Liar does to keep abreast of your schedule. If your partner has something major to hide, it stands to reason he'll want to know your every move before you make it. There's always a chance you'll run into someone who can supply you with some contradictory knowledge—someone who can blow the whistle on the deceit—and that's the last thing he wants to happen.

To understand how this gets played out in real life, assume, for example, you've gotten mixed up with a married man but you don't know he's married. The list of places where you might run into someone who knows his wife is a long one—hair salon, gymnasium, church, volunteer activity, just to name a few. If, on the other hand, your Romantic Liar is single, but he's lied about his background, he's still in the same boat. You could easily run into someone who knows the real story. Situations like that are always possible in the game of Romantic Deception, and those are situations that have to be managed. Simple translation? If the situation has to be managed, then you have to be managed.

With his need to know the ins and outs of your schedule at all times, a Romantic Liar will always want to know where you're going, who you're going with, who you might see and why. No detail of your schedule is inconsequential to a Romantic Liar. That's why he'll spend a lot of time *tending* to you. It's all a part of situation management.

The surest sign that you're being *tended* is you'll be getting a lot of telephone calls. You'll get phone calls at home; you'll get phone calls at work. You'll get telephone calls every day; you may get them every few hours. Lindy, for example, initially thought it was wonderful that her new boyfriend, Mitch, gave her a car phone as a present—wonderful until things got out of hand.

> *We'd been going together for about seven or eight weeks and Mitch gave me this car phone for my birthday. He said he'd just put it on his personal account*

and I wouldn't even have to pay the bill. Great, I thought. That's really sweet. Then it turned out to be a nightmare. I was working for a decorator back then, and I was all over town everyday. In a way it got downright spooky. I'd get in my car and Mitch would call. It got to where it was happening all the time. He'd want to know where I'd been, where I was going, when I'd be home—you name it, he wanted to know. I could never prove it, but I think he was checking on me 'cause he was married. I think it's real simple. He didn't want me running into his wife somewhere.

Apart from the sheer volume of telephone calls, it's the form the phone calls take that's so revealing. If the telephone calls you're getting have some identifiable, legitimate purpose, such as when and where the two of you will meet for dinner, what time the movie starts, whether you returned the library books you promised him you'd return, that's one thing. It's quite another, though, if the conversations always have to do with your personal schedule or plans and your partner's always asking about the *who, what, when,* and *where* of your day. Obviously tending doesn't always take place over the telephone. It's the same thing if your partner's always putting you through a mild inquisition when you're with him.

What a Romantic Liar knows about your personal schedule on a daily or hourly basis is still no guarantee he won't be exposed. On the other hand, any knowledge a Romantic Liar has about your daily life is better than none. Assuming something in your schedule signals potential exposure and your partner's quick enough on his feet (and most Romantic Liars are), he'll probably convince you to change your plans. There's no detail of your schedule too small for a Romantic Liar to consider.

Narrowing Tactics

If *tending behaviors* are designed for the short-term, day-to-day management of you and your life, *narrowing tactics* are directed toward a more long-term picture. *Narrowing tactics* are used by a Romantic Liar to limit your contact with the outside world in a significant sense. Remember: To a Romantic Liar, contradictory knowledge—anything that points to the underlying deception—can surface almost anytime, anywhere.

Of course, contradictory knowledge doesn't always have to come in the form of *factual* knowledge. Someone doesn't have to walk up to you and tell you he or she knows your partner is a liar. Sometimes all it takes is a shift in the way you've been looking at your relationship. Sometimes all it takes is a friend or family member who suggests maybe your partner isn't who or what he claims he is. Indeed, a large number of deceptive relationships start coming apart at the seams simply because the victim (often at the urging of a good friend) started looking at some small event in the relationship in a different light.

The unraveling process may start out with a victim's intuition kicking in because something doesn't make sense to her—something doesn't seem right or something doesn't fit. When the intuition kicks in, a lot of women start searching for a reality check—anything or anyone who can explain away the internal confusion. Most women will seek out someone—a friend or family member—and use him or her as a sounding board. In fact, women routinely turn to others to discuss relationships, particularly when there are some problems in the relationship.

Call it an expression of gender-based socialization if you want to, but it is a typical behavior pattern. I suspect that it's such a typical behavior that it's safe to say it is unusual for a woman to remain totally silent about relationship problems, at least when she's in the company of close friends. In fact, when a woman doesn't reach out for feedback from her friends in the face of what she thinks are some real questions about a relationship, that's more than just a little unusual. In fact, in cases like that I would say there's usually a reason why. In short, there's a very strong chance that she has been subjected to some *narrowing tactics.*

Assuming your partner's committed to keeping you snarled in a deceptive relationship, it stands to reason that he's also interested in restricting your access to sources of reality—anyone who would be in a position to offer an explanation as to what is really going on. It's one thing if some guy wants to keep you away from people who might have contradictory knowledge of a *factual* sort, but it's quite another if his aim is to control the way you look at reality. *Narrowing tactics* do just that; they represent an attempt to control your way of thinking and alter your sense of reality.

Here's an example to demonstrate the point. Let's assume the guy you've been seeing has lied about what he does for a living. Maybe he's told you he's a stockbroker but he really isn't working at all. It's one thing to deal with the chance that you'll meet up with someone who knows the guy really isn't working. The number of people who know the truth may be large, but it's a finite number. The number of people who could nudge you along the way to a reality check, on the other hand, is limitless. Even if you limit the pool to your close friends, family members, or coworkers, nobody in the group has to actually know for a fact he's not working. All they have to do is raise the possibility, particularly if you start talking about things like aspects of his schedule that don't make sense or the fact that you always get an answering machine when you call what you think is his office number. The same thing could apply no matter what sort of lies he has been telling you. All it takes is your intuition kicking in or some suspicions rising to the surface. All you have to do is have enough questions in your mind that you start asking others what they think. Once you do that you're but an inch away from someone telling you that maybe you ought to consider the relationship in a little different light.

Tending behaviors usually surface early on in a deceitful relationship, but *narrowing tactics* generally come later. As a matter of fact, they usually don't start until you're emotionally hooked. The reason should be obvious. Most Romantic Liars probably know that narrowing tactics cross over into the realm of controlling behaviors, and they probably also know that savvy women are apt to recognize them for what they are. Therefore, a Romantic Liar isn't apt to really unleash his narrowing tactics until you've been in the relationship for a while. A man who uses narrowing tactics early on in a relationship runs the risk of driving you away. Over time, however, narrowing tactics can easily be introduced into a relationship. If the process is subtle enough, you'll very likely not even sense what's going on. Even if you sense the dynamic, there's a chance you'll minimize or downplay the potential consequences.

When a Romantic Liar uses a narrowing tactic, it will almost always be an indirect act on his part. Yes, some Romantic Liars go so far as to issue edicts to their partners, telling them straight out, for example, that they're not to go out with friends after work, but most Romantic Liars are far more indirect when they play the game. Remember—the idea behind a narrowing tactic is to limit your contact with the outside world and your sources of reality testing. Here are some classic examples of narrowing tactics a Romantic Liar might use to constrict your realms of social contact:

- Criticizing your family, friends, or coworkers (e.g., saying derogatory things, making fun of them, belittling them, etc.)
- Suggesting you take time off from work to spend it with him
- Suggesting you quit your job
- Suggesting the two of you spend the evening alone whenever you suggest getting together with others (such as friends or family)
- Telling you he'd already made plans for the two of you if you tell him you were planning to meet with some friends after work
- Always having other plans in mind when you want to spend time with your family
- Asking who called if you get a phone call while he's at your place; showing some sign of displeasure because someone called you
- Criticizing leisure activities you generally do by yourself or with friends—going out to dinner, shopping, going to the gymnasium, going to movies, etc.

Any Romantic Liar who's committed to keeping the deception alive can ill-afford to have his target hanging around people who might urge her to look at the relationship in a totally different light. It should come as no shock then that Romantic Liars routinely make attempts to isolate their targets. Indeed, relationships based on deception routinely involve a woman who is systematically manipulated into a position of social isolation. It may start out slowly, but the isolation usually becomes a central element in the relationship. Gentle criticisms directed toward her family, friends, coworkers, or other associates characteristically become more biting, and the time she spends with others starts to decrease. The tactics may be subtle, but they're very powerful.

The fact that somebody uses tending behaviors to gain information about what you're doing and who you're with is probably less damaging in the long run than being the target of narrowing tactics. When a deceptive relationship comes to an end, you can look back on an avalanche of telephone calls and incessant questioning, put them in the nuisance category, and regard them collectively as action clues that were obvious, if only in hindsight. Recovery from the use of narrowing tactics isn't so easy.

Victims of Romantic Deception almost universally emerge from the experience with some of their more important past connections and relationships left fragmented, if not almost totally ruined or destroyed. Indeed, some women have severed ties with family and friends at the insistence of a Romantic Liar. Others add a job or meaningful career to the list of things they dropped at the urging of their partner. No matter how you slice it, the shattering of connections to your world of family, friendship, or work is far more injurious than the fallout from having to answer a bunch of phone calls or questions.

The Danger in Misreading the Action Clues Altogether

If you're someone who's misread the action clues in a deceptive relationship, you shouldn't feel alone. Hundreds of women make the same mistake every day. You don't have to be in a deceptive relationship to find yourself on the receiving end of *tending behaviors* or *narrowing tactics*. The same techniques are routinely used by all sorts of problem partners—alcoholics, drug abusers, as well as men who just happen to have a latent but serious dislike of women.

It shouldn't concern you in the least *why* someone uses tactics like the ones we've been discussing here. What should concern you is how and why the tactics work in the first place. In other words, the real question is *Why aren't a lot of women savvy enough to read the danger signals for what they are?*

A good part of the answer is found in the process of socialization. Women routinely misread tending behaviors and narrowing tactics because they look like something very different. Women routinely misread control tactics as signs of affection. It's nothing new. Patterns of socialization, along with a host of cultural clues, are at the heart of the misread. All you have to do is think about courtship and dating patterns—the rules of the game, as we call them—and you can begin to understand the influences of socialization and the larger culture. All you have to do is ask a simple question: *How does a woman know a man is interested in her? What do you expect a guy to do if he's interested in you?*

Chances are your response includes things like *he calls all the time just to say hello,* or *he wants us to spend all our free time together.* If those are the signs you expect to see out of a man who's trying to show some interest in you, it simply means you're pretty well tuned-in on our society's courtship and dating patterns.

When we look at them in the cold light of day, a lot of our society's courtship and dating patterns might strike us as a little silly, but the patterns are powerful. There are rules and expectations about everything from which party is supposed to initiate the relationship, how people are supposed to act on a date, and, in the case of what we're discussing here, what we're supposed to consider as outward signs of affection. Like I said, some of the informal rules and expectations may be totally irrational, if not downright silly, but they are part of the culture. To the extent that we buy the cultural messages—even down to the detail of learning what to take as a sign of affection—we get tuned-in on what the dating game is all about. In a word, we get socialized—we learn how the dating game is played. Signs of affection are just one more piece of the picture that gets defined for us—by our parents, by our friends, by actors in the movies, or by characters in romance novels, just to name a few.

It's little wonder then that a lot of women are likely to totally misread the clues. *He's calling all the time. Great! He wants us to spend all our time together. Great! He just wants to be alone with me. Great! That means he's interested.*

Because tending behaviors and narrowing tactics can so easily be masked or misinterpreted as signs of affection, any woman should have cause for concern. Maybe you find the whole idea a little repugnant because it has a way of dampening the thrill of romance, but you owe it to yourself to consider the thought. Your willingness to look at certain actions of your partner as a double-sided coin may be something you find extremely difficult to do. On the other hand, the pervasive nature of Romantic Deception should give you reason enough to try.

Obviously a man might be interested in you and give off some of the signs we've been discussing here—not for some sinister purpose, but because he's really crazy about you. Fine. A certain amount of that is normal. There's a point, though, when a healthy relationship comes up for air, so to speak. There's a time when each partner in a relationship deserves a measure of personal and psychological space. There's also a time when a couple on the road to a lasting relationship will want to include their circle of friends and family in their happiness. Obviously the key words are *healthy* and *lasting*. Relationships based on Romantic Deception aren't healthy, and they generally don't last.

The line is a fine one—when is an action, a gesture, or a spoken word an honest sign of affection or interest on the part of your new partner, and when is it a red flag? When do the signs point to a relationship that holds promise, and when do they point to danger? When is the guy absolutely crazy about you, and when is he just plain crazy? In the appendix of this book you'll find a list of things you can do to help you answer those questions.

As a matter of caution, I should tell you that the presence of action clues—whether it's the use of *tending behaviors* or *narrowing tactics*—is something that you should always take seriously. They are the signs of all sorts of problems ahead. What's more, a man doesn't have to be a Romantic Liar to rely on tending behaviors or narrowing tactics. He may be nothing more than a generalized control freak—someone who, for whatever reason, attempts to set the limits on anything and everything you do.

In the final analysis, it's not enough to just recognize tending behaviors and narrowing tactics when they surface. The critical question ultimately boils down to how you respond in the presence of them. If you mistakenly read them as signs of affection and remain silent on the issue (particularly in the face of narrowing tactics), you're asking for trouble. If you take a second false step by altering your own behavior in an attempt to please your partner, you might as well open the door and invite the misery to come on in.

The Fourth Sign: *So You Think It's Nearly Perfect*

I was crazy about him; my mom was crazy about him. All of it seemed too good to be true. I should have known something was wrong.

Marcie, age 34

Mack had me convinced he was my soul mate. Everything about him seemed perfect—the way he treated me—how we seemed to have so much in common. At least that's the way it started out.

Heather, age 29

The scary thing about all that was how safe I felt around him and how quick it happened. From the very beginning he had me thinking what we had was really special. It was like it was perfect—everything just clicked. I don't know how I got to thinking that meant I was safe, but I did. Just because you think you click with somebody doesn't mean you're safe.

Rachael, age 40

When you fall in love with a Romantic Liar, you're falling in love with an imaginary partner—someone who's not really who or what you think he is. So how is that possible? How is it that you could fall for a fake or a fraud? Certainly the information control and impression management you read about earlier are part of it, but there's also another factor in the equation, one that's absolutely essential in the launching of a deceptive relationship: the element of romance.

If deception is going to be successful, reality has to take a back seat. Something has to step in to block your perception of reality, and there's no better substitute for reality than a heavy dose of romance. If nothing else, Romantic Liars are big on romance. If you want to be wined and dined, look for a Romantic Liar. Nobody can top him.

When a deceptive relationship is unfolding, a Romantic Liar will use the information you've given him along the way to create an image that you'll probably find hard to resist. He draws you in with an image that's tailor-made for your consumption, and that's how the relationship is launched. But he keeps the relationship going by emphasizing romance. You think the relationship is nearly perfect, but there's so much that you really don't know.

Near Perfection Begins with an Emphasis on Image, Not Substance

Marcie, for example, thought Cliff was *finally the one* for her. Heather said the *attraction to Phil was immediate*. For Rachael, it was a case of *everything seemed right from the very first date*. In each case, the woman seemed to have so much in common with her new partner.

Unfortunately, like so many of the other women I interviewed, Marcie, Heather, and Rachael eventually found themselves trying to make sense of something that turned into a living hell. But that's not the way it started.

To understand why deceptive relationships come off looking wonderful at the outset, just think about how you evaluate relationships in the first place. If you are like most women, there are certain things you look for when you're initially judging someone as a potential partner. You're probably looking for someone with shared interests and values, a measure of physical attractiveness, a good sense of humor, attentiveness, politeness, and maybe the ability to be a good conversationalist. You might not be terribly systematic or comprehensive in how you go about your assessment, but still you'll be making judgements. In the process you'll determine that the right mix is there or it isn't. If the necessary ingredients are there, and your potential partner is willing, the relationship moves forward. It's as simple as that.

Of course, all that assumes you're in an honest relationship. In a case of Romantic Deception, all bets are off. You may think a potential partner has certain qualities or characteristics, but does he? Unfortunately, a Romantic Liar is capable of manufacturing nearly everything we're looking for, at least when you're getting to know him.

Aside from physical attractiveness and maybe a sense of humor, all the other factors on that list you just read can be faked, feigned, or totally misrepresented. For example, common interests and values can easily be faked or feigned. All it takes is someone who's willing to pepper a conversation with *me too* or *that's the way I feel, too.*

If you find it hard to imagine that someone would stoop to such a level, think of it this way. A Romantic Liar is someone who's more than willing to lie about all sorts of factual matters—where he was born, how many times he's been married, what he does for a living, and so forth. Given that, why wouldn't he just as easily lie about other things as well, including his attitudes, values, and beliefs? If he doesn't have to really back up any of his claims in those areas, who will know he's lying?

Only if we make it a practice to directly or indirectly challenge someone on what they are telling us do we have much hope of knowing the truth about anything. Yet few of us are likely to do that (for all the reasons I mentioned earlier). When it comes to the world of attitudes, values, and beliefs, even a direct challenge would likely lead us nowhere. You can question someone about their attitudes, values, and beliefs, but what does that tell you? The validity of an attitude, value, or belief is really only verified through a consistent course of action over time and in real-world situations—not in the throes of passion. And that brings us to the topic of romance. If there's anything that can stand in the way of living life in a realistic way, it's romance.

No doubt part of the seductive power of romance is found in the fact that romance takes us away from the real world of everyday life. Just think back over some of your own experiences. Surely you remember the feeling of being all caught up in the throes of romance. How many times were you in a relationship that seemed all too perfect until the romance started to wear off? How many times did you discover you and your partner weren't all that compatible once you got back into the real world and had to go about the business of living life on a day-to-day basis? Shared interests, mutual values, and compatible beliefs are only shared, mutual, and compatible when they're tested through time and in the real world of day-to-day living.

An Emphasis on Romance

It's really something of an understatement to say that romance transports you to a special world. For people caught up in the romantic experience, the real world comes to a near halt. Friends and family take a back seat to that newly discovered *one and only*, and there are all sorts of reasons why a long lunch over white wine and promises makes more sense than the world of work.

Particularly for women, the pull of the romantic experience is seductive. After all, it's wholly consistent with the myth of a Prince Charming we were introduced to as young girls. There'll be a time when he will arrive (or so the myth goes). He'll appear out of nowhere and he'll come to sweep us away. A perfect courtship; a perfect man; a perfect relationship. When we buy the myth, we buy the expectations.

If the romantic ritual is present, we're willing to believe. And in the case of Romantic Deception, you can count on the ritual. There'll be special times and special places. You'll celebrate your one-month anniversary, your two-month anniversary, and so forth and so on. You'll have a special restaurant and a special song. When it comes to the celebration of love, nobody does it quite like a Romantic Liar. In the aftermath of what turned out to be a horribly destructive relationship with a first-class liar, Kim described how Joe pursued her at the outset.

> *This guy was sending notes and cards in the mail within three days after we went out the first time. By the end of two weeks, he was signing them, 'with love, Joe.' I'll admit to being a sucker for romance. I fell for it.*

In the case of Phyllis, Sid's romantic pursuit bordered on being childlike, but it was effective.

> *At first I thought he was a little immature. He would show up with flowers; he even showed up with a box of chocolates. You know—stuff like that. What's weird though is how I ended up telling myself how sweet it was that he'd do stuff like that. I'll never do that again. All that romance stuff is great, but there's a limit. It can really get you into trouble. It's real easy to get everything out of perspective. I never thought I'd hear myself say this, but too much romance is dangerous.*

A Practical Need for Perfection

Even if we know what factors go into making a deceptive relationship appear so nearly perfect at the outset, that still doesn't explain why a Romantic Liar would want a relationship to have a look of near perfection to begin with. Although, we'll probably never know what really goes on inside the mind of a Romantic Liar, it's obvious that they have a very practical reason to make sure a relationship appears to be perfect. As Nicki, a woman in her late twenties, put it:

> *It has to seem perfect. It's as simple as that. If some guy's lying about a lot of stuff, he's got to make sure you're happy. Otherwise, all hell might break loose. Something goes wrong and there's no telling what you might do. You might go looking for him in the middle of the night. You might try to find him at work. Who knows what you might do. A guy who's lying has a vested interest in making sure you're totally satisfied with how things are going.*

In other words, success in the game of deception largely depends on the game's running very smoothly, if not perfectly. Alicia, who eventually learned to look at her relationship with Don in the cold light of day, took an almost analytical approach when she explained how he romanced her. She learned first-hand about why a deceptive relationship usually runs very smoothly at the outset.

> *I can look back on it now and see all of it in a different light. Call me jaded if you want to, but I think a lot of the way Don treated me was just part of the scheme. Remember—this guy didn't bother to tell me he was married. He told me he shared a condo with one of his buddies at work. Well, now when I look back on it, all his phone calls make sense. He'd call me at work, and he'd call me when I got home. I'll tell you another thing. He'd leave my place every night and he'd call me from his car phone. He'd tell me how much he enjoyed the evening and how he'd call me in the morning.*

> *There I was thinking this is a really caring guy. I imagine he just wanted to make certain I was in for the rest of the night and not following him home to where he really lived. If I had followed him home, I would have found out he was married, and the whole mess would have ended a lot sooner. But I didn't. I didn't have any reason to. He treated me great. He was the world's biggest liar, but he treated me great, if you can call it that.*

Up to the point that Alicia discovered Don was married, she thought everything was nearly perfect. Don showered her with affection; he was attentive to a fault; her wish was Don's command. It's very likely, though, that Don had some purpose behind much of his perfect partner façade. When all is said and done, it's probably time to modify the old saying about anything that seems too good to be true probably is. Maybe what we ought to say is *when it seems too good to be true, there's probably a reason why.*

The Fifth Sign: Patterns of Abuse

> *He was like a chameleon. When we started out he was real supportive—always telling me how proud he was of what I'd done and my career and all. But then it changed. All of a sudden he's saying things like 'that little job of yours' or 'I guess you have to go to work for that big, important meeting tomorrow'—real sarcastic stuff like that, and it worked.*

> *It worked 'cause I didn't stand up to him. I should have just told him he didn't have any idea what my job was like, but I didn't. I should have told him to get lost. But when you're all emotionally involved, you don't do that. That's the problem.*

> *Guys like those get a strong message when you*
> *don't tell them off. It's like you're giving them per-*
> *mission to take it to the next level. That's what*
> *Phil did. I guess I'm one of the lucky ones. The*
> *first time he hit me I called the cops. Four of them*
> *showed up at my door and they hauled him off.*
> *That did it for me.*

Kendra, age 32

Romantic Liars may be attractive and engaging at the outset of a relationship, but it's almost certain the façade will eventually fade away. Little by little, abusive behaviors rise to the surface and the relationship begins to take on a wholly different character. If your relationship with someone is taking a turn in that direction, there's a chance you're involved with a Romantic Liar.

Like many problem partners, Romantic Liars do a very good job at hiding their controlling and abusive tendencies during the initial stages of the relationship. Kendra's experience with Phil, for example, is very typical of what you can expect in a relationship with a Romantic Liar.

It is anyone's guess as to why there is an apparent link between deception and abuse, but the pattern repeats itself in too many cases of Romantic Deception to ignore it. Several explanations come to mind.

It may be that a partner's abusive behaviors are merely outward reactions to the internal stress that goes along with trying to maintain a false identity. You have to assume that anyone who goes through life making major misrepresentations to his intimate partner would have to feel some level of anxiety. It's not the lying that causes the stress; it's the threat of exposure. Since the potential of exposure lurks around every corner for a Romantic Liar, it's hard to imagine that the lid wouldn't eventually come off.

A second explanation for the abusive behavior that's so characteristic of a Romantic Liar is that it's simply a situation management technique—a means of ensuring that an unsuspecting partner stays on a short leash and remains in the dark. From this perspective, the controlling and abusive conduct of a Romantic Liar is merely an extension of the *narrowing tactics* you read about earlier—something he uses to keep his victims in line.

Finally, maybe Romantic Liars are men who have controlling, abusive personalities, and their controlling, abusive behaviors are simply part of their core personality. From this perspective, lying, as a form of *intellectual* abuse, is just one more form of abuse these men engage in. We generally don't think of lying as an expression of intellectual abuse, but that's exactly what it is. In fact, lying may be the most insidious form of abuse there is.

When all's said and done, of course, it shouldn't matter to you *why* your partner becomes abusive in the first place. The abuse is just another issue you're forced to deal with when you get involved with a Romantic Liar. Having to deal with someone who's lying to you should be enough. Add some abusive behaviors to the mix and you've got more than you ever bargained for. The best option is to exit the relationship as quickly as possible.

For some women, an involvement with a Romantic Liar approaches a near captive-like situation, one in which she has minimal contact with the outside world. It sounds like an extreme situation, and it is. But it's not all that uncommon in deceptive relationships. With the *tending* and *narrowing* in play, the situation becomes understandable if not predictable. When tending and narrowing is carried to an extreme, the result is something akin to a captive state. Since tending and narrowing are so instrumental to a Romantic Liar's success, it's little wonder that social isolation is frequently a part of a deceptive relationship. If tending and narrowing are good tactics for a Romantic Liar to use, social isolation is even better.

The significant amount of social isolation that is so characteristic of so many deceptive relationships creates an environment that's ripe for psychological abuse. When you're in a situation that affords you little or no contact with the outside world, you're highly vulnerable to what sociologists refer to as resocialization—a deliberate attempt to radically alter your identity. Indeed, successful resocialization is largely dependent upon some measure of psychological control and abuse. What Erica described gets to the heart of the matter:

*The same guy who started out with all these com-
pliments turned into a monster. At first I was the
prettiest, smartest, funniest woman he'd ever
known. He was real open about his feelings—he
couldn't get enough of me. By the time it was over,
though, he was a monster. He told me my life was
shit and he was the only one who could make it
any better. He told me I was fat and ugly and an
embarrassment. He told me my friends talked
about me behind my back and he was the only person I could trust. Little by little, he just beat me
down. I can't believe I let him do that.*

For Lynn, her experience with J.D. gave her a new understanding of what brainwashing is all about:

*You know what? This thing about these strange
religious cults? I used to hear stories about stuff
like that and I'd wonder how anybody could be so
stupid. I always figured somebody would have to be
real stupid to get sucked into something like that.
But now I know it can happen 'cause that's what it
was like with J.D.*

*I don't know how it happens, but I know part of it
starts when they get you all alone. I think that's a
big part of it. Before I knew what was happening,
J.D. had control over my whole life. It was like I
was a prisoner or something. I had to ask permission to do anything. It drove me crazy.*

*My father was dying, so I had to go back home to be
with him. My sister knew something was really
wrong with me—I guess I was acting like a nervous
wreck. She hammered on me pretty good—asking
'what's that guy doing to you?' She knew something
was wrong. When I finally broke loose from J.D., I*

*went back to stay with her and her husband. She
sort of patched me back together. She's the one you
ought to talk to—she saw it firsthand.*

As a rule, of course, patterns of abuse build up very slowly over
the course of a relationship, and it's rare they're recognized for what
they are when they first crop up. Only if you know what to look for
do you have any chance of figuring out what's really going on. You
owe it to yourself to be on guard against any expressions of control
or abuse. The simplest act of control should get your attention. Left
unanswered, acts of control usually escalate to acts of abuse. As a
guide, consider the following behaviors that Romantic Liars frequently exhibit:

Emotional and Psychological Control or Abuse

- Signaling you that your feelings aren't important (dis-
  counting or ignoring what you say, particularly when you
  want to express your feelings or ideas)
- Referring to you by demeaning or derogatory names
- Criticizing your friends or family
- Minimizing or making light of your accomplishments
- Making threats that he will commit suicide if you tell him
  you want to end the relationship
- Humiliating you in front of other people
- Asking or demanding that you alter your personal appearance
- Telling you that you will never reach your personal goals

Control and Abuse Using Intimidation, Threats, and Violence

- Physically abusing you by slapping, punching, shoving, or
  choking you
- Threatening to harm you if you leave him
- Telling you nobody can have you if he can't have you
- Driving recklessly when you're with him in a car
- Brandishing weapons around you

- Directing his anger toward physical objects (such as throwing objects or slamming doors in your presence)
- Destroying or damaging your property (home furnishings, your vehicle, etc.)

Characteristics of Controlling and Abusive Partners

It's not enough to recognize controlling and abusive behaviors when they're unfolding. The key is to see the signs in your partner before the behavior comes out. Here are some of the typical signs:

- *He voices support for traditional male-female role differences and stereotypes.* For example, he says things like *No woman of mine is going to work* or *I'm a traditional kind of guy and I just think men are the ones who ought to make the important decisions in a marriage.*
- *He has as a Jeckyl-and-Hyde personality and displays dramatic mood swings—he's one person one minute and someone totally different the next.* It's as if he's two different people. He can go from affection to near rage in the course of a few minutes, depending on what situation he's in.
- *He frequently abuses alcohol and/or drugs—even though you may not notice it at first.* Little by little, however, his use of alcohol is likely to increase in your presence. Even if he's not drinking in front of you, there'll likely be more and more occasions when he shows up at your place in an inebriated state.

A final word to the wise. Romantic Liars are characteristically controlling and abusive partners, but they're not the only problem partners that are out there. Domestic violence is very much a part of many relationships, including those that are without any sort of deception at all. At the first sign of excessive control or abuse, exit the relationship immediately. Don't wait around clinging to the hope that things will get better. All of the research shows it won't; in fact, it will only get worse. Just do it. Just leave.

The Sixth Sign: Intuition and Other Internal States

Most of what you've been reading up to this point has to do with what's going on around you—what your partner says (or doesn't say) and what he does (or doesn't do). Now it's time to look inside and shed some light on your internal states. When dealing with a Romantic Liar, everything inside of you, from your emotions to any sixth sense that you have, will be put to a test. The good news is that your internal states can be very instructive. Indeed, for many women, what was going on inside them became their first clue to the deception around them.

The Role of Intuition

Nearly every woman I interviewed spoke about how her intuition *told* her something wasn't right about her relationship with her partner. For some, the call from within came early in the relationship; for others, it was much later. Usually the women spoke as though they had no understanding of how intuition really works, but all of them had a healthy respect for it. Women who listened to their intuition early were glad they did. The others only wished they had paid attention sooner.

Intuition is something that almost defies rational understanding. Indeed, the essence of intuition is its lack of a rational basis. Most definitions of intuition emphasize three points. First, intuition involves an almost immediate processing or synthesizing of information. Whenever intuition overtakes us, it does so immediately and with no apparent warning. Second, intuition is generally thought to operate outside of or beneath the level of conscious reasoning. We usually think of intuition as a force or process that comes to our attention only after the processing has taken place. Finally, intuition normally defies our typical analytical approach in that it seems to seize on the whole of an experience first, rather than building a total picture from individual parts. When we sense our intuition, we sense a total picture but we don't know how the picture was assembled.

Consider what Justine said about the first time she went to Nick's house. It's a good example of how strong yet unstructured and incomprehensible our intuition can be.

> *I just got this really strange feeling. Everything about the house seemed too perfect. It was almost spooky. It was too neat—too orderly. More than that, it was the way Nick showed me around. He was opening closets and pulling out drawers—saying things like 'these are my socks, here are my suits,'—just stuff like that. The really weird part is that he said something like 'look here—see—I don't have anything to hide.' Well, it was just weird. I remember having a really strange reaction. It didn't make sense.*

As it turned out, Justine's experience was just an early indication of what was yet to come. Nick, as some later checking by Justine would confirm, had lied about everything from the number of times he'd been married to where he went to school and what degrees he had (or, rather, didn't have).

The way Justine described her intuitive experience was echoed by scores of other women. The situations that prompted the call from within varied, but there was a remarkable consistency in the way the experience was described.

> *It was just a voice inside—I can't describe it.*

> *Something told me there was something wrong.*

> *I got the strangest feeling—I couldn't put my finger on what was wrong, but I knew something wasn't right.*

Most of us know the feeling that comes over us when our intuition kicks in. It defies logic and it defies description, yet we feel its power. On the other hand, we sometimes choose to ignore it. And that was one of the questions that started to fascinate me while I was doing the research. I had heard story after story about how a woman's intuition became active, but I also heard story after story of women failing to heed the call. I wanted to look a little deeper, so I started asking the women why they didn't listen to their intuition in the first place.

A lot of the women said exactly what I expected: They didn't know why they ignored their intuition; they just did. Since intuition is something that operates outside of our rational faculties, that's a reasonable response. Sometimes it's hard to trust something we don't understand.

Other women were less unsure. They were very aware they'd pushed aside the intuitive messages, and they reasoned it was their emotional investment in the relationship that caused them to ignore the call. *It's real simple,* Genie said. *I didn't like what my intuition was telling me so I ignored it.*

Finally, there were the responses in yet a third category. In a way, they may have been the most interesting of the bunch. Janice's was typical.

> *I didn't listen to my intuition 'cause I didn't want to act like some irrational woman. You know—acting like something was wrong for no apparent reason. I didn't want to live out the stereotype of some kind of hysterical female.*

In a somewhat similar case, Shannon shut down her intuition when her family told her, in so many words, *to give it a rest!* Shannon was having second thoughts about her relationship with Richard, and she described those thoughts in a way that demonstrated how powerful intuitive feelings can be. In fact, Shannon voiced her feelings to her family during Sunday dinner with her parents and sister (Richard wasn't there), remarking that *there's just something about him that makes me wonder.* Unfortunately, the collective response of Shannon's family was to tell her what a nice man Richard was, adding that she *deserved a nice man for once in her life.* They thought she ought to lighten up and be glad she had a nice guy. Apparently Shannon's family didn't remember any of that when it came to light that Richard was actually married, but Shannon remembers the incident quite well.

The common theme that runs through the stories of women like Janice and Shannon is one of the social structure stepping in to shut down what could otherwise be a very powerful ally, at least in cases of Romantic Deception. For Janice, it was the familiar stereotype that women are irrational and prone to act all sorts of ways for no apparent reason. Janice was familiar with the stereotype, and she was sensitive to it. Intuition is all about reacting to feelings that surface for no apparent reason, so Janice fell victim to the stereotype. She didn't want to act like an irrational woman. For Shannon, it was the old and familiar message that a connection with a good man was a reward—something she deserved—and the message came from the people closest to her. Besides that, it was the same message she was receiving everywhere she looked—in the magazines, on the television screen, at the movies. Her intuition was trying to get her attention, but the competing voices won out.

The disturbing thing about all of this is that the very thing women are commonly thought to have more of—namely, intuition—often takes a back seat to stereotypes and social expectations. Of course, the notion that women have more intuition than men may be a stereotype in itself; I really don't know. It may be that women are simply more inclined to rely on it. Regardless of which sex, if either, is more equipped with intuition, the bottom line is the same for all of us. It's disturbing to think that such a valuable ally and powerful asset like intuition can so easily be dismissed.

Personally, I remain a firm believer in the power of intuition, particularly when it comes to cases of Romantic Deception. I've heard too many women tell too many stories about sensing something was wrong with the relationship. I've heard too many stories about how a voice inside was sending a signal—incomprehensible and nonspecific in any rational sort of way—but a powerful signal nonetheless. If there's a single best clue to a deceptive relationship, it's probably right there inside you. It's your intuition.

Cognitive Dissonance and Suspicions

If your intuition doesn't warn you, you logical faculties probably will. Eventually there will be some things you can actually point
to—things about your partner's behavior—that don't make sense.
It's what social psychologists refer to as cognitive dissonance—an
internal state that results when reality doesn't line up with your
expectations of reality. When you're in a state of cognitive dissonance, your mind gets more and more focused on one thing—
resolving the apparent inconsistencies. Eventually your mind will
start working overtime to lessen the confusion—sometimes to the
point that it becomes an obsession. Karen's effort to make sense of
Chuck's behavior is a good illustration of what it can be like:

> I guess I first got suspicious when he started show-
> ing up earlier and earlier at my place. He told me
> he was a marketing rep and he worked out of his
> apartment. When we started dating, he'd come by
> at night and we'd go out. After a couple of months,
> I gave him a key—really 'cause I wanted him to
> look after my cat while I was gone for a few days.
> Anyway, I told him to just keep the key.
>
> It wasn't long 'til I'd come home and Chuck would
> be there. He always had a reason—he was going to
> start dinner, he was going to fix something I
> needed fixed. He'd always have a reason. But
> eventually it got to where he was telling me he'd
> finished his calls and he just wanted to be there
> when I got home. Well that was fine 'til it started
> happening every day. Besides that, he got to where
> he was always showing up in jeans. No suit; no
> work slacks; just jeans. He'd tell me he finished his
> calls early so he decided to come by early.

> *After a week or so of that I started thinking something*
> *was wrong. I started thinking something didn't make*
> *sense. I mean I could understand it if he got off work*
> *early every now and then, but not all the time. I*
> *remember trying to convince myself he was just really*
> *good at what he did and that's why he finished early all*
> *the time; but then I started thinking about how he was*
> *dressed. I remember playing mind games with myself. I*
> *was with him about four months before I found out he*
> *wasn't working. He'd been lying all along.*

Our natural tendency is to work toward a resolution of the dissonance. Unfortunately, we sometimes take the easy way out. Instead of holding firm to our expectations of reality (e.g., *if this is* an honest relationship, then *this* is what would be happening), we downplay, minimize, or even deny the contradictory evidence. We put aside the reality by altering our perceptions.

In the world of Romantic Deception it's almost certain that you'll eventually find yourself in a state of cognitive dissonance. Something about your partner's behaviors—tangible evidence in the form of behaviors you can actually point to—will get your attention, and your suspicions will surface. Your intuition may have spoken to you earlier, but your intuitions were anything but grounded. When the suspicions crop up, however, your rational, logical faculties are engaged. That's when you'll start to notice events and actions that contradict your expectations. When you reach the state of cognitive dissonance, you've gone beyond mere intuition. You've also taken one more step toward going crazy.

Going Crazy

There's one last internal clue to a deceptive relationship that can hit you with an overwhelming force. It's the sense that you're going crazy and losing your mind. Feelings along those lines are as predictable as any other element of a deceptive relationship could be. Count on it: If you're involved with a Romantic Liar and the relationship goes on long enough, you'll eventually think you've lost your psychological bearings. You won't lose your connection with reality all at once; it's something that will happen over time.

When the thought that you've lost touch with reality sets in, you'll begin to feel a little anxious. The anxiety will eventually reach the point that you become confused and even a little frightened. The fact that you really don't understand what's going on is normal. Remember—when you're in a state of cognitive dissonance, your mind is working overtime. When your mind works overtime, but there's no resolution, the strain continues to mount. Even though the feeling can be overwhelming, it's not something that's beyond your understanding. It's a matter of looking at the underlying structure of the relationship you're in.

In terms of the way they're played out in the real world, deceptive relationships are tailor-made for craziness. By definition, deceptive relationships imply some disconnection between perception and expectation on the one hand, and reality on the other. Besides that, deceptive relations are ripe for confusion because they involve a partner whose actions frequently equate to what's referred to in the psychological community as *crazy-making behavior.*

When somebody engages in crazy-making behavior—whether that person is a romantic partner, a family member, a coworker, or a mere acquaintance—and the crazy-making is directed toward us, we find our sensibilities strained and our patience taxed to the limit. We sense we're being pushed into a corner because we can't find a rational way to deal with the person who's behind the crazy-making. If you really want to drive people crazy, here's how to do it:

- *Deny them access to clear and direct information.* Keep your responses to their questions vague and imprecise.
- *Send them contradictory messages.* Say one thing to them one day, but deny you ever said it the next.
- *Send them subtle messages (through your remarks or facial expressions) that their feelings or emotions or opinions have no importance.* Let them know that only your feelings, emotions, or opinions count.

- *Limit their personal space.* Make certain that they don't have a world apart from you—physically and emotionally.

All you have to do is read that list again and you'll see that all of those *crazy-making triggers* are almost always present in a deceptive relationship. First, a Romantic Liar isn't in a position to give you clear information. In fact, he's better served by giving you vague information. Second, a Romantic Liar also sends a lot of contradictory messages because his life is a contradiction. He says he's one thing when he really isn't. As to the third crazy-making trigger—signaling that your feelings and ideas are unimportant—Romantic Liars are well known for that very sort of thing, particularly when they're confronted. Finally, the fourth trigger—limiting someone's personal space—is very much a part of the *narrowing tactics* you read about earlier. In so many of the cases I listened to, the underlying dynamics were repeated over and over. It was as though the Romantic Liar had written a training manual on the essential elements of crazy-making. As for the women on the receiving end, it was like a descent into darkness where nothing made sense.

> *It didn't make any difference what I said or how I said it. Even when I knew I was right about something he would totally turn it around on me. I'd say something like 'you told me you were going to your mother's house last night.' He'd just look at me and say, 'I never said that.'*

> **Tara, age 31**

> *Here's how crazy it got. When I finally found out he was married, I went nuts. I screamed and yelled and told him I had spent half the afternoon talking to his wife. I was all upset. I said, 'How could you do something like this?' You know what he said? He said, 'Well, you were happy and she was happy.*

> *Why can't we just go back to the way it was yester-*
> *day when everybody was happy?' It was like I was*
> *trying to argue with a lunatic. He's sitting there*
> *acting likes he's lucid and rational and I'm think-*
> *ing I'm the one who's going crazy.*

Georgeann, age 29

A lot of the craziness that seems to surround a relationship with a Romantic Liar stems from the fact that they're constantly engaged in denials and deflections of all sorts. They say one thing one minute, but then they have to correct themselves the next to keep the deception alive. In addition to that, a lot of the craziness is linked to the fact that Romantic Liars have a way of telling lies that have a certain structure.

As any good attorney or student of philosophy will tell you, it is very difficult to *prove the negative;* it is very difficult to prove that something didn't happen the way someone said it did. And that's the position you'll find yourself in time and time again when you're dealing with a Romantic Liar.

For example, let's say that you're starting to get really suspicious about where your partner is at certain times, and you're starting to think that things aren't adding up. To bring some order to the confusion in your mind, you might have to prove that your partner *wasn't* really where he said he was at a certain time. If he says he was with friends, are you going to call them? You could—but would you?

If he claims he's a war hero, but you've got your doubts, how are you going to prove he's lying? It can be a tall order, as some of the women in my study found out. Here's one example:

> *Curt's war stories about all his secret missions finally*
> *got so far-fetched that I told him I wanted to see a*
> *copy of his service record. My ex-husband was in*
> *Vietnam, so I knew how important a service record is*
> *to a veteran. They really hang onto them 'cause they*
> *use them to get V.A. loans and stuff like that. It's*

called a DD-214; it's a record of everything a guy did in the service.

So I asked him to show me his DD-214. He looks at me with this blank stare and says, 'What do you mean?' I tell him I want to see his service record. I'm thinking this guy is a liar and I've got him against the wall. Nope; not a chance. He just looks me in the eye and says, 'There's no record 'cause I was in a special intelligence unit. What we were doing was so secret that there's no record of it.'

How do you deal with something like that? That's the kind of thing that will make you go nuts.

In a sense, the crazy-making behavior that's so characteristic of deceptive relationships represents the end of the psychological line, and it underscores how a relationship with a Romantic Liar can turn into a gradual descent into perceptual hell. First your intuition signals you, but you're likely to push it aside, for whatever reason. Then the more concrete suspicions surface, but they only serve to propel you into a state of cognitive dissonance. When the crazy-making behaviors come into the relationship, the downward spiral is accelerated. Throw in lies structured in a way that they're difficult to disprove, and you're there—immersed in a world where very little makes sense and where your grasp on reality is slipping away on a daily basis. It's testimony to what will eventually happen when you ignore your intuition and deny the cognitive dissonance. In the final analysis, your best clues to deceit are probably right inside of you.

SECTION IV

Some Things You Need to Know

If you're like most victims of Romantic Deception, you'll be in a relationship with a Romantic Liar for a good amount of time before you finally figure out what's wrong. Then, once you discover what's been going on, you'll be overwhelmed to the point that you'll have a lot of difficulty in figuring out what to do about it. At every step along the way you'll have the sensation that you're squarely in the middle of an emotional minefield, not knowing where to take your next step.

In the next few pages, we'll turn our attention to the ways out of a deceptive relationship and some of the things you can do to get your life back to a more normal state. We'll start with the question of how to assess your relationship in the first place. Then we'll deal with the issues of confrontations and other major mistakes. Finally, we'll turn our attention to the matter of disengaging from the relationship and reconnecting with the world.

Any serious connection with a Romantic Liar will likely be a trauma-inducing experience, and the psychological dimensions of a traumatic experience are never to be taken lightly. Recovery is rarely quick and, as you'll soon discover, it won't be easy. The good news, though, is that a recovery and return to a normal and rewarding life is possible.

Assessing Your Relationship

As a rule, the problems inherent in a relationship with a Romantic Liar continue to mount, and his behavior will become more and more mysterious as time goes on. If you're like most victims of Romantic Deception, you'll also be focusing inward and examining each and every aspect of *your own behavior*—wondering if there is something in your behavior that's causing all the problems.

It's a maddening experience—having to deal with an increasing number of problem behaviors coming out of your partner, but not having a clue why things are spiraling out of control. The sad thing about all this is that the explanation is so simple. If you only knew your partner was lying, everything would begin to make sense. The fact that he's been lying would be the key that unlocks the door to all the mystery.

Unfortunately, a lot of women delay the ultimate realization of what's really going on because they fail to make an honest assessment of their relationship. Either they don't know what to look for, or if they do they're unwilling to take the step. As for you—and assuming you've read this far, everything that's necessary to push you toward the realization is in place—you know what behaviors to look for, and you know it's time you paid attention to your intuition and suspicions. You also know that a lot of the evidence is probably right in front of you. But the question is *Will you act? Will you do what's necessary to make an objective assessment of your situation? Will you entertain the thought that you've been lied to on a big-time basis?*

If you're like a lot of women, you'll very likely hesitate—for days, for weeks, or maybe for months. Even that is understandable—self-destructive, perhaps, but understandable. From start to finish, deceptive relationships are intense. When they're good, they're great, but when they're bad, they're a living hell. It's only natural then that you'll find yourself on an emotional roller coaster when you get involved with a Romantic Liar. The longer the relationship goes on, the more extreme the emotional swings will get. The end result is you'll find it very difficult to look at anything about your relationship in an objective fashion. The emotional highs and lows, if they're allowed to go on long enough, will eventually impair your ability to think rationally.

That means you won't be able to accurately assess your personal situation until you have a grip on your emotions. If you're involved with a Romantic Liar and you're ever going to figure that out, your emotions are going to have to take a back seat. In a word or two, you'll have to have your rational faculties about you. Here are a few things to remember.

Respect Your Limitations

Accept the fact that you might not be able to make an objective assessment of the situation on your own. If you're emotionally tied to your partner and you're emotionally invested in the relationship, you may need an outsider or two to keep you on track. If you have any doubts about your abilities to really look at your relationship in an objective fashion, call on family or friends or someone else you can trust.

If you're so far into a deceptive relationship that you're estranged from family and friends, make an honest effort to re-establish your contact. When you're attempting to re-establish the contact, make certain you're honest when you reach out for help. You should be willing to openly discuss how it came about that you gradually lost contact in the first place. The *how* and *why* behind your social isolation is valuable information for you and anybody else who might be in a position to help you.

If you don't feel comfortable asking family or close friends for help, turn to a therapist, a counselor, a social worker, or another member of the therapeutic community. If you think you need help to be objective, get it. Your goal is to gain a better understanding of the relationship you're in.

Remind Yourself of What It Means to Be Objective

Before you look at your relationship, take the time to remind yourself of what it means to be objective. Remind yourself that first and foremost, being objective means you'll look at *the totality* of the relationship. It means you won't dismiss or downplay the suspicions you have, and it also means you won't tell yourself the good outweighs the bad. When the time comes to do something like write down everything you know about your partner and whether or not you think it's true and why, you have to be willing to be honest. Objectivity starts with honesty.

Look for Patterns

If you're going to assess the totality of your relationship, you have to look for *patterns*. When you only focus on isolated incidents (what your partner said or did at this time or that), you lose perspective. What you want to look for are recurring patterns of behavior that can point to a deceptive relationship. For example, if your partner *always or frequently* changes the subject when you ask him direct questions, that's a pattern. If you're *rarely or never* able to reach him at certain times of the day or night, that's a pattern. It's also a pattern if his calls to your office or home are so *predictable and frequent* that you can tell time by the ringing of the telephone.

Don't Let Your Defenses Get in the Way

If you won't allow yourself to look at the totality of your partner's behavior, you might as well forget making an assessment in the first place. The same thing is true if you are willing to consider the full range of your partner's behavior, but you persist in making excuses, finding justifications, or conjuring up plausible explanations for the things that trouble you. If you find you're having trouble, reread the section on asking others to help you. Also, consider the fact that you're probably relying on some common defense mechanisms, such as these:

- *Rationalization*—telling yourself that if he's lying, he's only doing it to impress you or to keep from hurting you; telling yourself that you're the one who will cause him to change his behavior
- *Selective Perception*—only focusing on the good aspects of the relationship and not even acknowledging the bad; pushing aside your suspicions; ignoring the evidence in front of you
- *Intellectualization*—acknowledging the bad aspects of the relationship (and the possibility that he's been lying to you), but telling yourself that the emotional tradeoff is worth it

Start with the Stages and Go from There

Assuming you can keep your assessment objective, start by rereading the material on the different stages of a deceptive relationship. Reread it with an eye toward what signs to expect at which stage and which signs apply to your relationship. At the same time, always remember that the stages in a deceptive relationship aren't always clear-cut or neatly defined. One stage blends into another, and depending on the particular dynamics of your relationship, you could find you've skipped a stage or that you move back and forth between different stages at different times. It's an excellent way to open the door to reality—an excellent way to get you thinking about how long the madness has been going on.

Also go back to the section on the various clues to deception. Make mental notes of the different behaviors to look for, along with the sensations inside you that might be signaling a deceptive relationship. Remember—the idea is to be objective. The idea is to give honest answers.

Assessment Versus Action

Let's assume for a moment that your assessment of your partner's behavior and the overall relationship leads you to conclude
that you're mixed up with a Romantic Liar. Maybe you now have
the incontrovertible evidence in front of you. It's only natural
that you'll have a strong emotional reaction. You'll be depressed.
You'll be angry, maybe even to the point of harboring some
homicidal fantasies. You could also experience strong feelings of
jealousy (particularly if your partner's lied when he told you that
you're the only one in his life). In the face of overwhelming
emotions, your inclination may be to act immediately. *Don't!*
You can act quickly—in fact you should. But quick action doesn't
necessarily mean immediate action.

Immediate actions are likely to be impulsive actions. They
spring from strong emotions like anger and the sense of betrayal.
What you should be looking for are actions that are well thought
out and measured. Even those can be quick actions, but they're
not impulsive.

Certainly if you find yourself in any stage of a deceptive relationship and there's abuse involved—either verbal or physical—
you'll want to act very quickly. Even if you haven't discovered
any deception, abuse of any form in any relationship should be
enough to point you toward an exit. Just remember—the more
immediate the need to exit a relationship, the *smarter* the exit
should be. If that means calling on friends, family, counselors, or
shelters, do it.

The Problem with Confrontations

The dynamics of Romantic Deception almost guarantee that
you'll want to confront your partner. Assuming there's no longer
any doubt in you mind about whether or not your partner's been
lying to you, there's a better than even chance that you want to confront him. Look at all the other negative emotions you've suffered
as a result of deception in the first place—shame, embarrassment,

and depression, just to name a few. And think about everything else he's put you through—wasted time, depleted emotional resources, maybe even some job or career setbacks. That's enough for anyone to endure. More than likely you'll share some of the feelings some of the women in my study expressed:

> *I just wanted that son-of-a-bitch to know he couldn't get away with it. I couldn't stand the fact that he'd made a fool out of me. He'd ruined my life, and I wasn't just going to sit there and take it.*
>
> **Tina, age 41**

> *After what he'd put me through? He deserved to be told he was a piece of shit.*
>
> **Regina, age 35**

> *I was totally humiliated. I mean, I couldn't even face my friends. I wanted to get even.*
>
> **Toni, age 28**

Even though your own feelings may echo some of those same words, it's a good idea to keep in mind that confrontations with Romantic Liars don't work. I repeat: *A confrontation isn't going to work. There's no such thing as a successful confrontation with a Romantic Liar.* Besides that, a confrontation with a Romantic Liar can be dangerous, so the risk is doubly foolish. There'll never be a satisfactory resolution.

Rather than drawing your partner into a confrontation, you're far better off asking yourself what you expect to get out of a confrontation in the first place. Better yet, ask yourself how you would define a *successful* confrontation. If your partner is a Romantic Liar and you think a confrontation will change his behavior, forget it. A confrontation won't cause a rebirth of his character, and it won't cause him to emerge as a changed man, totally given to truth-telling. It's *not* going to happen.

Fundamental character flaws are tough to modify under the best of circumstances, and they're not going to be repaired just because you pushed the confrontation button. Confront a Romantic Liar with the fact he's been lying to you, and here's what you can expect:

- He'll stop you in midstream and not let you follow through; he'll change the subject or turn your attention to other matters. For example, he'll try to get you focused on a trip you're planning to take or an anniversary you're about to celebrate; he'll tell you he needs your support if he's going to land that new job, etc.
- He'll choose to ignore you, taking a path of quick retreat, disappearing from the scene for a few days or weeks. If he adopts the quick-retreat strategy, he'll very likely return in a few days or weeks, perhaps in the hope that you will have somehow forgotten about all the lies.
- He'll explain his way out of the confrontation by telling you more lies (except you probably won't know they're lies at the time he's telling them). If he adopts this strategy, you'll probably not know this is what he's done until the haunting feelings surface in your mind again.
- He'll turn the confrontation around on you, suggesting that you're always trying to start an argument. This sort of strategy only promotes more confusion in your mind. It is crazy-making behavior writ large.
- He'll deny he ever said or did any of the things you're accusing him of saying or doing. This is still another behavior that promotes your internal sense of confusion.
- He'll react in an equally confrontational manner, maybe to the point of getting abusive. The chance of receiving a confrontational reaction from your partner is simply too great to risk.

As I said, there's no such thing as a successful confrontation with a Romantic Liar. You are far better off to exit the relationship as swiftly as possible, saying as little as possible. Certainly you can expect a partner to attempt to contact you, if only to ask what is going on. Just prepare yourself for what may follow.

He may show up at your work, your home, or anywhere else he thinks he can find you. He may contact your friends in the hope he can convince them to convince you that it was all a big misunderstanding. You should let your friends know in advance that you don't want to see or hear from your partner again. Whatever it takes to steel yourself against your partner's re-entry into your life, you should do it. The bottom line is that you never owe an explanation to a Romantic Liar. After all he's done to you, you don't owe him anything.

If nothing else, a Romantic Liar's lying should be a strong signal to you that he's the type of person who's willing to operate outside of social convention. It's a sign that he's fully capable of bending or breaking some important rules of behavior. When you're dealing with a rule bender or rule breaker, issues of your personal safety come into play. The fact that you think people are supposed to be nice to one another and refrain from abusive behavior has nothing to do with a situation like a confrontation with a Romantic Liar. Remember—thoughts like those are nothing more than thoughts you hold. They have absolutely nothing to do with how a Romantic Liar views the world.

The fact that Romantic Liars are known to get abusive is something you should keep uppermost in your mind, particularly if you're thinking about a confrontation. Remember what I said earlier. It's worth repeating over and over: *There's no such thing as a successful confrontation.* Your emotions may be giving you a strong push toward a confrontation—so strong a push that you find it hard to resist—but fight the urge. Your safety is at stake. Just to summarize, here's a list of things you should always remember when you think about confronting a Romantic Liar.

- Romantic Liars who have shown abusive tendencies in the past will very likely show signs of hostility when you confront them about their lying.

- Even a partner who has never shown any outward signs of abusive or hostile behavior can reveal that side of his personality when you accuse him.

- When you confront a Romantic Liar, his hostilities can run the gambit. He might limit his response to verbal abuse, but he might just as easily react with an outburst of physical abuse, as well.

- Destruction of your possessions or property is a common reaction to a confrontation, particularly if you use the confrontation as a means of telling him you're going to leave him. The mere fact that you confront him with his lies may also trigger a rage-like response simply because he knows that he has been exposed. Depending on the extent of his lies and the extent to which he fears you might expose the truth to others, his response can easily reach a point that puts you at a long-term risk. Many Romantic Liars follow up their initial outburst of anger with extended campaigns of retaliation that include stalking and harassment directed toward a victim while she's at work or out in public. Some women have confronted Romantic Liars and thought they simply went away quietly, only to learn that the worst was yet to come.

In the final analysis, the less you say about the reasoning behind your decision to leave him, the better.

The Other Major Mistake: Thinking You're Going to Change Him

While a confrontation would be a big mistake, there's still another mistake that may be even more harmful to your overall well-being. It's your desire to know *why* your partner lied to you in the first place. More than any other question you'll ask, the question of *why* will haunt you from the moment you discover the deception until you finally put the relationship to rest.

Wanting an answer to why an intimate partner was so willing to breach your trust is normal and natural. Even if you've dealt with problem partners before, the fact that someone lied to you will probably strike you as the most grievous transgression possible. The act of lying is an assault on your integrity. It leaves you with an overwhelming sense of betrayal and the feeling that you've just gone through an emotional train wreck. If you're like many victims of Romantic Deception, you'll eventually reach a state of near obsession in your desire to know why. Still, you need to keep in mind that this might not be a healthy desire. It all depends on the reasons behind your search for an answer.

If you're driven to find an answer because you want to arrive at some sense of closure on the relationship, that's probably a legitimate reason, though I'm not totally certain of what the word *closure* really means. If, on the other hand, you're not certain what's driving you in your search for an answer, I urge you to be very cautious. At a minimum, you should spend a little time asking yourself *why you want to know why* in the first place. If you're inclined to think that knowing why your partner lied to you will eventually put you in a position to change his behavior, forget it. You couldn't make a bigger mistake.

The minute you cross the line into that way of thinking, you only invite more problems. All it does is fill you with a false sense of hope—one that convinces you that you'll eventually change the behavior of a Romantic Liar, provided you can just find out what motivates him in the first place. To say that thinking along these lines is unfounded is an understatement. It's roughly equivalent to thinking that you've got some powers that far exceed those of the therapeutic community at large. After all, what you're telling yourself when you start thinking thoughts like this is that you're going to rehabilitate someone who's got some major character flaws.

Allowing yourself to think that you're going to change your partner is fundamentally egotistical, if not downright arrogant. Trained therapists find it extremely difficult to even deal with big-time liars, let alone successfully treat them. For you to think that you're going to transform somebody with serious character flaws may be as delusional as the life your partner is leading. In the final analysis, it may be one of the most self-deceptive thoughts you could have.

The Right Question to Ask

If you're ill-advised to spend too much time trying to find an answer to the question why your partner chose to lie to you, what are your options? If it's become a near obsession with you, how do you find a way out of the mental morass?

The road out is a pretty straight one. Instead of asking *why your partner lies,* ask yourself *why you tell the truth.* Once you do that, you'll most likely begin to experience an inner transformation that will give you the strength you need to leave the destructive relationship.

Once you squarely face the issue of why you tell the truth and why you put such a premium on honesty to begin with, you take the first step toward accepting what's happened to you. The mere act of asking yourself why you tell the truth draws all the issues to the fore. Here's what is apt to happen as soon as you shift the focus by asking an altogether different question:

- You begin to understand how important honesty is to you and why it is one of your fundamental values.
- You begin to understand what happens when trust is broken and why character in a partner is essential if a relationship is to have substance.
- You begin to understand what it means to have a value conflict, and you begin to understand that a relationship that lacks mutually shared core values is a relationship destined for failure.
- You begin to understand how different you and your partner really are and why the relationship has no future.

Asking yourself why you tell the truth will likely allow you to see—maybe for the first time—the full measure of your partner's lack of integrity. More important, perhaps, it might allow you to once again understand who you really are—despite any efforts your partner may have made to redefine you and your world. Here's how Tess describes her epiphany:

> *I struggled with my feelings for a long time. I did everything wrong I could do. I denied what was going on and I tried to make the feelings go away. I had fallen in love with this man, and all the feelings had taken over. The truth was inside me, but I didn't want to face it. I guess I just had to get so miserable that there wasn't any other choice. And that's what I did.*
>
> *I started asking myself what I was doing. I started asking myself why I could fall for somebody who was so different from me. I forced myself to think about how different our values were. That's when it started to change. That's when I got it together enough to leave him. It was like some kind of emotional breakthrough. I finally started thinking about myself. Up 'til then all I did was try to make it work. He was sick; the relationship was sick; it wasn't going to work.*

Disengaging and Reconnecting

You can make the decision to end the relationship and even go so far as to tell yourself that you're going to stick to your decision come hell or high water, but that doesn't mean you'll necessarily follow through on your first try. Victims of a deceptive relationship routinely find that it's very difficult to exit the relationship and make the exit permanent on their initial attempt. Don't let that fact overwhelm you. There are reasons why the exit isn't easy.

We can start with the obvious—your life has probably been thrown into a tailspin by your encounter. Chances are you're in an emotional state that you've never experienced before, so there's a reason why you might not be able to immediately muster the rational faculties an exit will require.

Not only is a familiar relationship coming to an end, you're probably awash in a sea of betrayal. Sensing a multitude of emotions hitting you from every direction, you'll probably have difficulty trying to determine which end is up. From the outset you'll be hit by a recurring thought pattern—one minute thinking about what your partner meant to you and then realizing the next minute that he wasn't that person to begin with. It's as though your mind is playing tricks on you. As much as you know you should end the relationship, the false picture of your partner—the man you thought he was—will enter your thoughts to push you back toward him.

Your recovery begins when you take the steps to once again engage your rational side and force yourself to look at the relationship objectively. To do that, there's one fact you're going to have to face: The relationship you've been in was an unhealthy one, because it was based on anything but honesty. It may have had a lot of physical intimacy connected with it, but genuine emotional honesty wasn't present. Remember—the goal at this point is to return to objective thinking. The more you can accept the fact that the relationship was unhealthy, the more quickly you become objective.

If you need some convincing that you've been involved in an unhealthy relationship, take a look at the list below. It's an encapsulated enumeration of what often takes place when you try to disengage from an unhealthy relationship. Read the list, and ask yourself just how many items apply to what you've been experiencing. It's a good starting point because it will get you on the road to *acknowledging* what you're really dealing with as you move to leave your relationship for good.

- You're finding it difficult to emotionally disengage from the relationship, even though your rational side is telling

you that the relationship is hopeless and the damage can't
be repaired.

- You spend endless hours blaming yourself for the problems in the relationship. You tell yourself that things will
get better if you can be more understanding.

- You're constantly telling yourself that your partner is going
to change, or worse yet, you're telling yourself that you're
the one who will bring about the change in his behavior.

- You can't accept the thought of ending the relationship
without becoming fearful or anxious about what your life
will be like in the future.

- You continue to look at your relationship as something
that is directly linked to your emotional or financial well-
being. You can't imagine a life of sufficient emotional or
financial resources without your partner at your side.

The idea at this point is to acknowledge what's been going
on and come to the realization that the relationship is
unhealthy. If you're unwilling to accept how truly unhealthy the
relationship is, you're destined to forever redefine it as something you can *fix*.

For all the reasons I mentioned earlier, you should never
allow the deception to continue by telling yourself that you can
change a Romantic Liar. It amounts to self-deception of the
worst sort. If you have to read and reread the signs of an
unhealthy relationship until you're willing to accept the true
nature of your relationship, do it.

The Predictable Reactions

Simply acknowledging that you've been in a fundamentally
unhealthy relationship doesn't end the emotional nightmare. It
only brings you closer to reality. You still have to deal with a cas-
cade of powerful emotions.

The emotional reactions to an experience of Romantic
Deception are usually quite extreme, and victims routinely

describe it as a form of intellectual or emotional rape. The sense of betrayal that accompanies an experience of Romantic Deception can be overwhelming. Your inclination will be to keep the experience very private, and the personal sense of embarrassment and humiliation may steer you in that direction. Don't take your feelings underground. Remember that you're not alone. You're going through what thousands of other women have gone through as well.

Recovery Won't Be Immediate

Your power to recover from an experience of Romantic Deception will largely be influenced by your acceptance of a basic principle: Recovery won't be immediate. It will take time, and it will take effort on your part. If you expect to recover immediately, you only prolong the process. Here's the rule to remember: *Give yourself time to recover.*

When you give yourself time to recover, you do two important things. First, you resist the temptation to immediately rush into another relationship. When you're trying to disengage from an unhealthy relationship, the last thing you need to do is rush headlong into another relationship, healthy or otherwise. You've got a lot of work to do—soul-searching, important work—and you owe it to yourself to do the work in a way that has your full attention. There's no way you can go about the work of recovery if you're immediately rushing into a new relationship. Second, giving yourself time to recover gives you the chance to become aware of your *recovery gains* on a daily basis.

You can want and hope and even expect your life to return to normal in a short time, but that's not likely to happen. If you go into the recovery process with an expectation of immediate success, you only set yourself up for defeat. If you mistakenly assume that your progress will be immediate and obvious, but it doesn't unfold that way, all you'll be thinking about are the losses. What's more, you won't see any of the gains.

If, on the other hand, you give yourself time to recover, the small gains you'll be making on a daily basis will have a lot of meaning. The ability once again to enjoy the company of friends, return to an exercise routine, or approach your work with enthusiasm can take on significant meaning, provided you take the time to let the process work. Paula's story is a powerful one in that regard:

> *I don't think I'll ever forget how it affected me. I went into a depression that totally immobilized me. I was suicidal. It was all I could do to get out of bed in the morning and get to work. I'd come home and go to bed. I didn't have any energy. On the weekends, I'd just stay inside with the curtains shut.*
>
> *I finally told myself that I had to do something— even if it meant I just walked down to the end of my block and back. I had to do something, so that's what I did. I made myself do the same thing later the same day. Then I told myself I had to do that the next day after I got home from work.*
>
> *After a while, I was walking another block and then another. I turned it into an exercise thing. It wasn't real serious exercise, but it worked. It worked. That's all I can say. You don't know how horrible it was—the depression and hurt. I hate to think what I might have done if I hadn't taken that first step.*

Bringing the Real Relationship into Focus

Think about another relationship you had trouble ending; now double or triple the pain. That's Romantic Deception. The reason has a lot to do with the tricks your mind is still playing on you. You were very much involved with someone and now the relationship is over. There's only one problem. The person you were in love with really didn't exist. In a situation like that, your mind has no choice but to do flip-flops on you.

The image you were in love with was very powerful—powerful enough to attract your love and commitment. An image like that isn't going to go away overnight. Your emotional side won't let it. On the other hand, your rational side now knows that the image you were in love with didn't exist—at least not in reality. Now your rational side pulls at you. And so the flip-flop goes— your emotional side one minute, your rational side the next. To get beyond the tricks your mind is playing on you, focus on what is going on inside your mind. Acknowledge to yourself that your mind is seesawing between fantasy and reality. Don't dismiss what is going on. Better yet, use what is going on inside your mind to your advantage. Whenever you find your thoughts going back to your partner as the man *you thought he was,* tell yourself that you're very aware of what's going on in your mind. Then focus on *your partner as he really is.*

The Different Emotions You May Experience

You may have experienced intense emotional reactions to the dissolution of a relationship before, but remember, the termination of a deceptive relationship is qualitatively and significantly different. Your intimate imposter was not who or what he claimed to be. In a situation like that, it's little wonder that you'd end up all over the emotional map. It's essential that you tackle your feelings in a positive manner so you can move on and put the ordeal behind you. Here are three important things to remember when dealing with your emotional reactions to the experience of deception:

1. Don't bury or suppress your feelings—they will eventually surface in one way or another.
2. Acknowledge that your feelings are legitimate—you have every right to feel the way you do.

3. Remind yourself that you are in control—you have a choice on how to deal with your emotions.

Here are some of the more typical emotional reactions you can expect.

Depression

Clinical depression is a common mental health problem—one that is estimated to affect more than fifteen million people in our society at any given time. Roughly fifteen million more would be classified as having a mild form of depression at the same time. It is estimated that approximately one out of six persons will go through a major episode of depression at some point in his or her lifetime. Those numbers alone should convince you that depression is a common problem.

Depression is largely described in terms of how it affects both your moods and behaviors. It can range from the more normal depressive episodes (particularly when they are tied to an event such as the loss of a loved one) to major depression, which is usually characterized by a significant or profound sense of despair and hopelessness. Sometimes the depression is present but only noticeable in symptoms of significant changes in weight, insomnia, irritability, and so forth.

The potential seriousness of depression cannot be overemphasized. Suicidal thought patterns are common in cases of clinical depression, and the estimates of how many clinically depressed persons eventually attempt suicide are alarming. There is, however, a very positive aspect to all this: Depression can be treated very successfully. Many sufferers are able to return to a normal life within relatively short order, provided they get the treatment they need. Treatment plans based on psychotherapy, medication, or some combination of the two are found to be highly successful for millions of sufferers. Appropriate treatment actually begins when you recognize the symptoms of depression for what they are.

All of us experience periods of sadness or moodiness at various times throughout our lives, but depression is an altogether different emotional state. Some level of depression is a common reaction to the end of a significant emotional relationship, so the fact that you are likely to experience a bout with depression shouldn't surprise you. On the other hand, you don't want to totally dismiss any of the feelings that accompany a depressive episode. It's important to monitor the true extent of any feelings you might experience. Here are some of the more typical signs of depression:

- Feelings of despair, hopelessness, and gloom
- Recurring feelings of sadness or distress
- A loss of interest in doing things that you enjoy (extracurricular activities, hobbies, etc.)
- Difficulty in sleeping and an interruption in your normal sleep patterns (insomnia, oversleeping, fitful periods of interrupted sleep, etc.)
- Changes in dietary habits (a loss of appetite and accompanying weight loss, or an increased appetite and weight gain)
- Difficulty concentrating, making decisions, or trying to remember things
- Recurring thoughts about suicide
- Feelings of restlessness, worthlessness, irritability, and helplessness
- Feelings of fatigue and an inability to go about your daily routine with a normal amount of energy or interest

As I mentioned, depression is a normal reaction to an emotional loss of any sort, and many people find that the experience of depression subsides and their lives return to normal within a relatively short time. Likewise, many people are able to overcome their depression through a self-directed program of minor life changes. For example, some of the things you might rely on to move forward in the face of an episode of depression include the following:

- Forcing yourself to make social contact with friends and family
- Getting involved in new activities such as volunteering or joining organizations, enrolling in educational courses, etc.

- Changing your daily routine or habits
- Starting an exercise program or consciously increasing your exercise regime
- Taking steps to improve your diet and making certain that you get a sufficient amount of rest

Having said all that, I would also re-emphasize that some bouts of depression can be more serious than others. An experience of depression can last a few days or weeks, but it can also last longer. Not only that, sometimes the symptoms become extremely severe and the consequences can be self-defeating, if not self-destructive. If you have the slightest inclination that what you're dealing with is more than a mild or temporary case of depression, it's time to seek some professional help.

Remember—the feelings are normal, but they can be powerful. In the face of a more pronounced episode of depression it's foolish to assume you can deal with it on your own. Take the necessary steps to find help, whether you call your physician, a mental health clinic, a crisis hotline, a family member, or a close friend. Take some *active* steps to find help. Don't just wonder if you should seek help or think about getting it.

Anger

Anger is a common reaction to injustice. When someone has dealt you an injustice, it is normal to feel a sense of anger. To the extent that you have gone through your life operating on the assumption that a significant partner should be honest, some feelings of anger are to be expected.

If you can accept the fact that your reaction to the injustice is normal, you'll be in a better position to deal with your anger in a positive way. By accepting the fact that the anger is normal you're not denying it; you're simply acknowledging it. Once you've done that, you can begin to deal with your anger by rechanneling your energies in the right direction.

Though your natural feelings push you toward a constant replaying of the relationship in your mind, resist the urge.

There's nothing to be gained by spending countless hours look-ing back over the relationship and rewriting the outcome (what you would do differently). When you constantly replay the rela-tionship, you only stall your recovery. Worse yet, you can easily convince yourself into thinking you can return to your partner and start the relationship anew.

By the same token, don't allow yourself to hold grudges or thoughts of revenge against your former partner. Not only are grudges and revenge fantasies dangerous, they take your focus off of the important party—you. Finally, don't allow the anger to push you toward self-pity and self-doubt. If you sense feelings like these, acknowledge them by reminding yourself that you know what is going on with your emotions. The more you learn to sense, identify, and acknowledge your feelings, the greater your power to change them.

Betrayal

A lot of people and situations can make us angry, but the injustice that gives rise to anger is compounded when it's dealt by someone close to us or it occurs in the context of a significant attachment. When that happens, we feel betrayed.

The experience of betrayal can be life-altering, causing you to question everything about your life. For many of the women I interviewed, the experience of Romantic Deception had caused them to doubt their ability to accurately judge the character of other people. Many also found that they had started questioning many of the beliefs they had held throughout their lives—beliefs in values like honesty and truthfulness. Still others begin to entirely lose faith in the idea that it is possible to find a connec-tion with a partner who won't eventually deal them some signifi-cant misery.

Those are feelings that aren't easy to overcome. Realistically, there is little that can be done to alleviate them in an immediate sense. Recovery from a sense of betrayal is something that takes time because it takes exposure to situations in which honesty and truthfulness are demonstrated. Because of that, it is vitally important that you move forward from an experience of Romantic Deception with a *measured attitude*—an attitude that doesn't shut the door to future relationships, but an attitude that reflects an appropriate amount of caution.

The worst thing you can do when you're trying to move forward is to immediately get involved in another relationship. Don't even hope for that in the immediate future. Yes, recovery will take time, but *time,* by itself, isn't the healing agent. What will eventually heal you is your exposure to those situations I mentioned—situations in which honesty and truthfulness are *demonstrated* to you by the people around you. Situations like that are most likely made available by family and close friends, and that's why a reconnection with others is so important to you. There's no greater healing agent than a connection with someone you know you can trust.

Shame, Embarrassment, and Humiliation

Apart from the anger and feelings of betrayal, some measure of embarrassment, shame, or humiliation is only natural. You were duped. You were hoodwinked. Somebody put one over on you. It's as simple as that. It doesn't matter what led up to it or how he pulled it off. Those are merely the details. The bottom line is that you were taken in by a Romantic Liar.

Embarrassment is an emotion that goes along with feeling self-conscious. *Shame* is a term that we often use to describe a particularly strong sense of embarrassment. Humiliation is a feeling that is connected with a loss of our pride or dignity. One sensation that seems to run through each of those—embarrassment, shame, or humiliation—is the notion of an audience of onlookers, real or imaginary.

When we feel embarrassment, shame, or humiliation, a lot of the discomfort comes from the thought that others are looking at us and judging our behavior. These audience-related emotions, as I like to call them, can indeed be powerful. If they're particularly strong, they can cause us to retreat to whatever private place we can find. These are the feelings that can cause us to closet ourselves away from the rest of the world, just when contact with others is really what we need most of all.

For some women, feelings along these lines were connected to their recognition that they were part of a larger charade that involved still other people (for example, women who got involved with married men, especially married men who had children). Lisa's story is a case in point:

> *I'd grown up with this vision in my head about women that date married men. Then I woke up and saw it was me in that picture. I was disgusted. I was disgusted at myself. I was horrified that I had been the woman in that picture. He had two children at home. God, I was horrified at what I had done.*

> *I called his wife because I was ashamed of what I had done. I wanted her to know that I'd really thought he was divorced. That's what he told me, and I believed him. I wouldn't want some woman messing around with my husband if I was married. That's just the way I am. I think she finally believed me, but I don't know. At least I had the guts to call her.*

Other women are beset with the range of audience-related emotions because they begin to imagine how their friends or family would react if they told them about their partner's true nature and how they were deceived. For an audience-related emotion to take hold, all that is necessary is the image of an audience in your mind. The image can be rooted in reality or it can be totally imaginary; it makes no difference.

When feelings like those we've been discussing start creeping in, remind yourself of two important points. First, Romantic Deception is something that happens to thousands of women every day. You're not the first woman who's been through the experience, and you won't be the last. Romantic Deception is an unfortunate fact of life. Second, always remind yourself that what you're feeling is really an expression of your emotional vitality—a demonstration that you do have feelings and emotions and values. The chances are very good that the Romantic Liar who was part of your life has great difficulty in feeling anything—including embarrassment, shame, or humiliation.

Other Emotional Reactions

Some women who have been through an experience of Romantic Deception describe their reactions in terms that emphasize an overwhelming feeling of anxiety or, at times, near panic. Common symptoms include hyperventilation, rapid thoughts, fatigue, and confusion. In some of the more dramatic cases, the women describe symptoms that are highly characteristic of post-traumatic stress disorder (or PTSD). For example, many women describe a wide range of symptoms such as a generalized numbing of emotions, a detachment or estrangement from others, a difficulty in concentration, an interruption of normal sleep patterns, and irritability.

As in some cases of depression, the experience of anxiety can be very normal. Indeed, it can be argued that a certain amount of anxiety can be a positive force, particularly when it serves to keep us away from dangerous situations or when it causes us to take an extra step to be prepared for some task that we face. On the other hand (and again, similar to some cases of depression), some cases of anxiety, if left untreated, can have debilitating consequences. A generalized anxiety disorder is said to be present when symptoms such as fatigue, headaches, tension, and excessive worry are present for extended periods of time.

It is safe to say that reactions along those lines can reasonably be linked to some of the dynamics that seem to be a familiar element in deceptive relationships. Certainly the elements of control and abuse that are so routinely found in deceptive relationships could trigger reactions that range from anxiety to panic—and beyond, for that matter. And the fact that victims of deceptive relationships frequently are socially isolated cannot be ignored when looking for triggers of a PTSD-type reaction.

Once again, however, anxiety and panic disorders, along with PTSD, can be successfully treated, but it is essential that the treatment be carried out with the assistance of a qualified mental health professional. Should you have the slightest thought that you may be experiencing unusual levels of anxiety or any of the specific symptoms mentioned here, you should seek out competent diagnosis and treatment.

And Then There's Denial

Denial is a defense mechanism—something we reach for when the pain is too much to endure. Denial allows us to translate a real but painful experience into different terms—placing it in a different context. If the pain or loss that results from a deceptive experience is too great, you may opt for some level of denial.

You're apt to engage in denial at any number of places along the road of Romantic Deception. It's possible, for example, that your failure to listen to your intuition early on was some form of denial, and denial could have been operating when you started working overtime to make sense out of so many of your partner's confusing and contradictory behaviors.

Your denial is also apt to operate when you begin disengaging from the relationship. For example, you might be engaging in some denial if you try to convince yourself that you're leaving the relationship for reasons that have nothing to do with the deception. Maybe you're telling yourself that you're finally going to leave because of the abuse or because you think the relationship is going nowhere. In a practical sense, these are very legitimate reasons to leave. Whatever it takes to get you going out the door is positive. But don't let denial like that linger too long.

Bring it to the surface; acknowledge it. Admit to yourself what really happened. Accept the fact that someone was able to deceive you. It's essential if you want to protect yourself from a repeat performance somewhere down the road.

Don't Bury or Suppress Your Feelings

If you choose to bury or suppress your emotions, they'll only become more deeply embedded within you. What's more, they'll likely come out at a later date. It could be weeks or months later, but the chances are that you will eventually experience anger or rage or depression. Even under the best of circumstances, an experience of Romantic Deception (like any significant act of betrayal) can result in symptoms rising to the surface that border on post traumatic shock disorder—reason enough to begin the process of acknowledging your feelings early on.

You may also find that your physical health begins to suffer when you try to suppress your feelings. When your physical well-being is in jeopardy, your emotional well-being is only further undermined. In the long run, you're far better off if you will acknowledge your feelings at the front end of the disengagement process. Accept the fact that you have some serious emotional work to do.

Fears and Other Roadblocks

Disengagement from a relationship (deceptive or otherwise) often gives rise to any number of fears. An intimate involvement with someone has a way of mixing all sorts of elements into a stew—entangling lives, aspirations, assets, and any number of other considerations. With disengagement, however, *doubt* becomes the word of the day—doubt about what is going to happen to you now and in the future. Depending on how long you were involved with your partner, your doubts can turn into fears. There are three main types described here.

Security Fears

Because Romantic Liars tend to be abusive—some of them achieving the status of a batterer—you may find yourself facing some very real fears about your personal security. There is no single issue more important to your overall well-being than a safe exit from an abusive or potentially dangerous partner. All other fears should take a back seat to any security fears you have. There is no point in worrying about where you might be living or working in the future if your safety is in jeopardy.

Any exit from an abusive relationship should be approached with considerable thought. You may be in a position to make a swift, sudden, and secure departure (for example, you might be able to move in with friends or family), but you may find that you don't have those options. You may also find yourself realistically worried about whether or not moving in with friends or family would put them in jeopardy at the hands of an openly hostile partner—all the more reason why any exit from an abusive relationship demands considerable thought.

Help is available. Most telephone directories now carry the telephone number of domestic abuse shelters, suicide prevention/crisis hotlines, and counseling centers. If you find yourself stranded, get to the nearest telephone and contact your local police department or a crisis hotline. All of these resources can get you pointed in the right direction. If you have the slightest inclination to call a resource of any sort, make the call.

Emotional and Relationship Fears

It's only natural that you would wonder how long the emotional turmoil will last and what's ahead for you in the way of future relationships. Having fallen for a big-time liar, you'll probably have some questions about your ability to accurately judge potential partners. It's important that you resist the temptation to adopt the conventional wisdom and blame yourself for what happened.

Give yourself some time away from any sort of long-term, serious relationship, but use the time productively. Use the time to work on your own well-being, and use the time to educate yourself about the signs of deception. Other relationships will come in time.

Resource Fears

You may have quit your job; you may have taken up residence with your partner. Worse yet, your partner may have gained control over whatever financial resources you have or had. The result is that you may end up seriously wondering how you can afford to leave the relationship, even though you want to. A true testimony to the degree of control that Romantic Liars exercise over their partners, many women seriously question how they're going to survive.

Resource fears are immediate and tangible. When they're present, you live with them every moment, often to the point that you view them as overwhelming obstacles. Can you get a job? Will you make enough money to live? How will you get transportation to work? What about child care? Where are you going to live? Those are very real issues that have a way of turning into fears. As overwhelming as some of those fears may seem, you can deal with them.

Turning Your Fears into Questions

Whether you're dealing with emotional or resource fears, it's important that you not let your fears get the best of you. It's healthy to acknowledge your fears, but don't let them rule you. One way to keep your fears from overtaking you is to approach them as questions. The key words in the process are *options, opportunities,* and *choices.*

For example, if you're faced with having to find a new place to live because you were living with your partner, move beyond the fear stage by turning it into a question. List your options. If need be, list short-term and long-term options. Write down the options; discuss them with friends or family members; ask for their advice.

If you've quit your job because your partner told you he was going to take care of you for the rest of your life, use the same approach. Think about opportunities; list your options. If need be, ask yourself where you'd like to work, what you'd like to do, what's the best way to locate the right job, and so forth. Once you immerse yourself in questions—and then you force yourself to answer them—the order to your life will start to return.

The same sort of approach applies if you're facing some relationship fears. For example, you can spend some very productive time asking yourself what you expect in a partner and how you intend to approach relationships in the future. The simple act of writing down questions and answers can do you a world of good. It's an excellent way to keep your rational faculties engaged.

Developing a Sense of Control

Another key element in a successful recovery from an experience of Romantic Deception is your ability to regain control of your life. You may not have had control of your partner's decision to deceive you, but you do have control over the way you put your life back together. If you sense that you've lost control of who you are or where you're going, concentrate on the following:

- Remind yourself that your feelings aren't going to go away overnight, and then commit yourself to a course of constructive actions that focus on you and your healing.
- Remind yourself that you will experience all sorts of emotions. Instead of allowing yourself to be overwhelmed by them, concentrate on what the emotions are signaling to you. When the emotions surface, take mental note of them. Have conversations with yourself about what the emotions are signaling and why they are present.
- Remind yourself that over time the feelings and emotions connected to the experience of Romantic Deception will eventually fade.

- Finally, spend some directed energy in telling yourself that it's OK to be selfish and focused on yourself. Spend time and energy thinking about what it means to take care of yourself and act accordingly.

A Serious Warning

Even though there are ways to constructively deal with any number of fears when it comes to disengaging from a deceptive relationship, I would be doing you a serious injustice if I didn't emphasize the need for caution. The picture I've tried to paint of many Romantic Liars should be a familiar one to you by now. In addition to lying on a big-time basis, Romantic Liars frequently are unpredictable, moody, and controlling (often to the point of being downright abusive). Many have drug and alcohol addictions, along with any number of other self-destructive traits. For some Romantic Liars, the lying is the least of their problems.

Because Romantic Liars tend to be problem partners of the first order, there's no such thing as a guaranteed easy exit from a deceptive relationship. It's true that the longer you've been involved with a Romantic Liar, the more problematic your exit from the relationship is apt to be. But even a short-term involvement is no guarantee you'll get out unscathed. All a short-term involvement with a Romantic Liar means is that you know even less about him than you would had you been involved for a longer time. That's a pretty scary notion when you think about it.

Obviously, I don't suggest that you hang around a Romantic Liar a little longer to figure out what you think is the best way to leave him. At the first sign of deceit you should exit the relationship. On the other hand, it's always a good idea to have your wits about you. Lydia's story is a case in point.

❧❧❧

About two months into her relationship with Hank, Lydia discovered he'd presented her with a resume that was pretty much a fake from top to bottom. For Lydia there wasn't any thinking to be done. She wasn't accustomed to dealing with liars and she didn't plan to start with Hank. On the other hand, she didn't see any reason to be rude or confrontational. She figured a straightforward but polite approach would be the right one.

Lydia called Hank at work. She told him that she'd been thinking it over and the relationship wasn't going anywhere. She also told Hank that she didn't want to see him again. When he pressed her for more details, Lydia let him know she'd found out he'd been lying to her.

Maybe Hank didn't like getting the news that the relationship was over. Maybe he didn't like the fact that his lies had been exposed. Either way, what Lydia thought would be an easy end to a relationship brought out a side of Hank she'd never seen before. In fact, she would have never predicted it.

The stream of phone calls started later that night, so Lydia just let the calls mount up on her answering machine. When the pleas that she talk things over went unanswered, Hank escalated to name calling. By midnight, he was making threats. Two days later, Hank was waiting by her car when Lydia got off work. Hank's direct harassment didn't let up until Lydia got a restraining order.

❧❧❧

When I talked to her (some two years after the breakup), Lydia still wasn't sure she'd seen or heard the last of Hank. He was still driving past her office every now and then, and she was certain she'd seen him hanging around the building where she was taking a night class. Lydia, who thought she was taking the right approach when she let Hank know he'd been found out, would be the first to tell you she didn't have a clue what sort of person she was really dealing with.

Truth be known, there's no assurance that any approach would have been the right one with a character like Hank. For example, had she waited for Hank to call her (rather than calling him at work), he *might* have taken the news in a more mature way, but there is no guarantee. And that's the lesson in Lydia's story. When you're dealing with a Romantic Liar, you really have no idea what you're really dealing with in the first place. And that's why any exit from the relationship should be approached with caution. In the interest of your own safety, here are a few things you should always remember when you get ready to leave a Romantic Liar.

- Romantic Liars who have shown abusive tendencies in the past will very likely show signs of hostility when you end the relationship.
- Even partners who have never shown any outward signs of abusive or hostile behavior can reveal that side of their personality when you decide to say good-bye.
- In some cases, Romantic Liars simply disappear from the scene when they're found out, but it is not something you should count on. We can only surmise what really motivates a Romantic Liar to begin with. The fact that a Romantic Liar is found out may only present a challenge to him—the challenge of getting you to take him back.
- The hostilities shown by a rejected Romantic Liar can run the gamut. Some stop with verbal abuse, but many react with an outburst of physical abuse, as well. Destruction of your possessions or property is a common reaction to a breakup, as well as stalking and harassment directed toward you while you're at work.

Bringing Voice to Your Experience

By now you know there are certain themes that I've tried to stress throughout this book. One of them is that every case of Romantic Deception is unique—a situation made unique by the individuals involved, the relational setting in which the deception occurred, and the specific lies that were told. Unique situations are, by definition, sometimes difficult to understand, so you cannot assume that those around you will necessarily understand what you've been through.

You may have friends or acquaintances who've also experienced their own entanglement with a Romantic Liar, but that doesn't mean that they will necessarily understand your unique situation. Therefore, you should always remind yourself of what you're up against when you break your silence.

You don't have to take out a full-page ad in the local newspaper to explain what happened to you, but you do have to *give voice to your experience.* By giving voice to your experience, I mean you have to let your true feelings come to the surface. If you're like most victims of Romantic Deception, you'll naturally be reluctant to talk to too many people about what happened. Nobody likes to admit they've been duped, fooled, or taken advantage of, so your reluctance is understandable. But bottled up reluctance does you no good; in fact, it can do you a lot of harm.

If you're initially reluctant to openly discuss the experience with someone else, that's OK (at least for a while), but you still need to get the thoughts and feelings out in the open. If you're inclined, you can have a one-sided, private conversation with the Romantic Liar who led you down the primrose path. You can scream, yell, curse, and throw things if you want to. Just do it in private. Pretend your former partner is there and he's having to listen. If you want to write him a letter, that's fine, too. But don't send it. Just write the letter, read it back to yourself a few times, and put it away in a place where you can always go back to it. You'll probably be amazed at your reactions to your own words after a week, a month, a few more months, and so forth. You'll know the healing process is underway when you sense that each time you read the letter the intensity of your emotional reaction is lessening.

Don't Expect Everyone to Listen Without Criticism

Once you begin to *give voice to your experience*, you'll be waking up some of your most fundamental emotions, and the fact that you were betrayed will likely be on the top of the list. In a situation like that, you can ill afford to risk any sort of secondary wounding in the form of people telling you the experience was really your fault in the first place.

Given that, you should be aware that a lot of people think Romantic Deception always requires a willing victim. That's just the way they see the world. They may be perfectly wonderful folks in many respects, but they have a tendency to turn the blame around on the victim. You don't have to avoid people like that altogether, but you're well advised to look elsewhere when it's time to openly discuss what you've been through.

Choose Your Audience and Setting Wisely

When you decide to talk to someone about your experience, you'll want to talk with someone who's very *special*—a family member, a very good friend (as opposed to a mere acquaintance), or someone in the counseling profession. At the heart of the issue is your sense of trust. That's why you'll want to turn to someone like a trusted friend or a value-neutral professional—someone who will take the time to listen to what you have to say and someone who is willing to listen without judgement.

You'll also want to choose the right setting. It always pays to remember: There's no such thing as a simple case of Romantic Deception. As a rule, a complete *telling* of an experience can take hours. If you make the decision to talk to a counselor of some sort, you should count on several visits just to get it all out in the open. If you're planning to talk to a close friend, don't plan to do it over lunch, drinks, or any sort of hurried setting. Find the right time—when your friend will have plenty of time to spend with you—and find the right place—somewhere you can feel comfortable.

Learning from Your Experience

An exit from a deceptive relationship is something positive, but it is only of lasting value if you learn from the experience. In the appendix of this book you'll find some practical exercises and activities you might want to consider the next time you find yourself drawn to a potential partner. There's also a lot of practical information that can help you find out a lot of facts about your partner before you get too involved. Before you get to that part of the book, though, there's a certain amount of emotional learning you'll want to think about. The practical learning is important, but so is the emotional.

When it comes to emotional learning, one of the best places to start is with a solid understanding of what your rights are as an individual. When you regard your rights as paramount, you gain a much clearer definition of who you are and what you should expect from others.

First, you have the right to make mistakes—big mistakes and little ones. You also have the right to correct mistakes and move forward, putting your mistakes behind you. By the same token, you have the right to set your own goals and modify them as you move forward. It's your choice whether you let other people help you clarify those goals along the way or whether you want to set your own course totally on your own. You certainly have the right to reject others' suggestions when they tell you to put aside your personal goals and aspirations altogether.

It's also your right to trust your intuition and your system of values. Along those lines, you have the right to say *no* to situations and people who don't seem right or circumstances that make you feel uncomfortable in any way. When it comes to matters of principle, you have every right to take the high moral ground, decline the invitation to debate, and never look back.

You also have every right to expect and accept nothing less than a healthy partner. A healthy partner is one who encourages you toward your goals and doesn't stand in your way of reaching them. It's also a partner who is capable of disagreeing with you without being destructive to the relationship. Healthy partners aren't abusive; they don't threaten or demean or harm you.

Finally, a healthy partner is honest. He is a man of character who believes in telling the truth. When it comes to letting you know who and what he is, he doesn't misrepresent, fabricate, keep secret, or deny the facts of his life. A healthy partner isn't beset with that insane level of arrogance or arrogant form of insanity that earns him the label of Romantic Liar. No, a healthy partner is one secure enough in his identity and self-image that he has no need for Romantic Deception.

Final Thoughts

After countless hours spent listening to tales of Romantic Deception, the topic still intrigues me as much as it did when I started the project—maybe even more so. The mystery and illusion that is so much a part of Romantic Deception is something I still find fascinating. Practicality suggests I eventually have to stop collecting stories, but I still find it impossible to totally shut the door of inquiry when yet another woman steps forward to tell her story about the man who deceived her. I suspect that's the way it's going to be for some time. I'll continue to collect stories and see where they lead.

Every time I think I've heard the last word, another Romantic Deception story comes along to remind me how much remains unanswered. Still, there has to be a temporary halt to the collection of stories, and I have to face what may be the biggest questions of them all: *What does all of this tell us about the way life gets lived in our society? What does all this say about the future of relationships?* In the end, I can't be all that optimistic. I say that for any number of reasons.

First, so much of the way Romantic Deception gets played out in real life almost ensures that it will forever be an *individual problem* for *individual women*. When all is said and done, I don't expect the larger society to ever get too worked up about

Romantic Deception. The phenomenon of people lying to their intimate partners isn't likely to ever rise to the level of a full-blown socially-defined social problem. As individuals, we may find it repugnant that someone would totally misrepresent who or what he is in the context of an intimate relationship, but those are just our feelings and reactions as individuals. And individual reactions aren't likely to hold much weight against the power of a conventional wisdom that's so heavily steeped in the tradition of blaming the victim. As long as the larger society can write off Romantic Deception as a phenomenon that's largely the result of the victim's mistakes, we will remain just as we are today—never giving much thought to the *actions of Romantic Liars*. As long as we overlook or totally ignore the apparent lapse in character that is so much a part of a Romantic Liar's personality, we will forever be cut off from what may be the biggest question of all: *What does it mean to live in a society where deception can and does take place at every level, even the most intimate?*

In a curious sort of circular dynamic, most victims of Romantic Deception will probably remain very silent in any public sense, and their silence, in turn, will simply fuel the conventional wisdom that paints them as women who invited the deceit in the first place. Books like this can be written and read by a lot of women, but there's no guarantee the result will be any sort of large-scale, wide-spread public concern about honesty in intimate relationships. Instead, I suspect the conventional wisdom will remain alive and well. The finger of blame will be pointed toward the victim, and the perpetrator—the Romantic Liar—will go about his business without much criticism from the larger social order.

In that sense, I'm inclined to conclude that Romantic Deception will remain nothing more or less than one more dirty little secret about the way life gets lived in our society—one more case of repugnant, reprehensible behavior that is defined as something a victim invited. Additionally, I doubt seriously that the public wants much of a debate on the topic of Romantic Deception. Any recognition that Romantic Deception is something that's fairly pervasive would have some serious downsides. For starters, I doubt our society really wants to contemplate what it means to live in a world where you could, at any moment, discover that your most intimate partner is an impostor. I dare say that widespread recognition of that possibility could bring us to the brink of societal insanity.

I also suspect that Romantic Deception will be with us for quite a while simply because *it works*. In the simplest of terms, Romantic Deception makes it possible for some pairings to take place that otherwise might not. Something as simple as a lie here and a misrepresentation there makes it possible for some people to be who and what they are not—more available, more interesting, and maybe more desirable than they really are. As long as our dating and courtship rules define *in advance* what our partner is supposed to be like there will be people willing to do lots of things to meet those expectations, even if it means they have to circumvent the rules by telling a few lies.

On a more positive note, there will always be a significant proportion of the population going about dating and mate selection with a commitment to honesty—people who know that real intimacy is always based on honesty and truthfulness. There will always be men of character and integrity, secure enough in their own identities that they have no interest in creating illusions for themselves or those around them.

For others, however, Romantic Deception will always be an easy option. After all, it takes only a lie here, a misrepresentation there. Indeed, for some men Romantic Deception may be an extremely attractive option. In fact, for some, Romantic Deception may be the obvious choice—something akin to the grand embodiment of the American Dream—the chance to be a self-made man, if only in some sort of narcissistic, twisted sense. After all, with Romantic Deception on his side, a man can be who and whatever he wants to be.

APPENDIX

Survival Guide

Advice from Other Women

At the end of most interviews, I asked the women if they had any advice for other women—what they would say to other women who were involved in the dating scene. I thought the responses might give me some indication of whether or not the experience of Romantic Deception had changed the way the women went about meeting and getting to know the men they might date. Also, assuming the women actually offered some specific suggestions, I thought the information might be useful to others.

The question turned out to be very revealing. The responses I got were as telling as any of the larger stories I've reported in the previous pages. I've taken the liberty of including a lot of their suggestions here—they're as important as any other thing that I could tell you.

- *Run a background check on him. It's as simple as that.*
- *Get him around your friends and keep him around your friends.*
- *Approach dating the same way you would if you were interviewing for a job or hiring somebody to fix something for you. Ask a lot of questions.*

- *If he always wants to come to your house, there's something wrong. If he really doesn't have any friends, there's something wrong. If he materializes out of thin air and there's nobody around him—no close friends, nobody he hangs out with— that's a tip-off.*
- *When he starts telling you a bunch of stuff right off the bat, it's a sign something isn't right. If he reels it off like a resume, there's something wrong.*
- *If a guy has some kind of job where he doesn't have a normal work schedule, it's a red flag. If you don't meet his family members in a real family situation and you don't have a chance to really sit down and talk to them—that's another flag.*
- *I tell you what I look for in a guy now. When I'm around him the first few times, I look for crisp answers. You know what I mean. When I ask him a question about where he works or where he grew up and stuff like that, I want a crisp answer.*
- *I don't know if I'd have a guy checked out or anything like that. I guess I just don't want to get totally paranoid. But I'll tell you what I would do. It's what I do now. I won't go out with anybody unless I know somebody that knows him pretty well. I just won't do it. It's too easy to get fooled. It's not worth it.*
- *I don't know how many times I've heard somebody say you have to take the time to know somebody. Well, it's true. It's real easy to get all infatuated and hop into bed and think you've got true love working. But that's not love and all of us know it. I don't know why we don't take the time. Maybe we're afraid of what we'll find out.*
- *I guess I really don't like to admit it, but I'd have the guy checked out. I know what it's like to get mixed up with a big-time liar, and I know how smooth they can be. I've worked too hard for what I have, and I don't plan to risk it. I have friends who spend more time researching where they're going on their next vacation than they do on the guys they date. I wish 'em luck.*
- *If you're going to be open with him, he should be open with you. If you tell him you're going to make sure he's telling you the truth—if you tell him you're going to check him out—and*

he can't handle it, tell him to get lost. If you've been hurt before and he can't handle that, he's not worth it.

- I really don't think it's too much to ask to see the divorce papers. I know papers can be fabricated, so I'd say go ahead and look it up at the courthouse. I'd look it up at the courthouse even if some guy showed me the papers. If he has a problem with it, that's tough.

- If a man doesn't give you a home number and a work number and he wants to call all the shots, I'd wonder about that right off the bat.

- If he doesn't give you a home number, there's something wrong. He's married. Even if he gives you a home number, he still might be married. You have to go to his house or apartment or wherever he lives. If that's not happening, something is wrong.

- I'd either do the checking myself or hire somebody to do it. So what if it takes a little time or effort. So you spend fifty or a hundred or two hundred bucks. So what. You might spend that in a heartbeat—buying some new clothes just to impress him. Make the investment. It could save you a lot of heartache in the long run.

- I wouldn't trust a guy even if one of my friends introduced me to him. How do I know that he hasn't totally put one over on them? I don't care how I met him or where I met him, I'd have somebody do a background check on him.

- I used to be sort of a wimp, but not anymore. When I meet somebody, I ask all sorts of direct questions. And I expect direct answers. Now I pay a lot more attention to exactly what a guy says. If he says he got divorced a couple of years ago, that's not good enough. I want to know the exact year. I want to know the circumstances.

- I'd say listen to your intuition. Somebody can tell you all sorts of things. He can even give you detailed answers—unbelievably detailed answers—but that doesn't mean he's telling you the truth. It's your intuition. Intuition is something that can cut through that stuff if you'll let it.

- I'd tell other women to look for anything odd about the relationship. Absolutely anything. If something doesn't add up, there's

something wrong. If he doesn't want to give you a home number.
If he says you can't reach him at work. If he's vague in things he
tells you about the past. Stuff like that should tip you off. Where
we go wrong is we try to excuse the things that don't make sense.
We try to come up with something in our minds that will make it
make sense. If there's something odd, it's a signal.

Partly as a result of comments like these and partly because
of the other findings that surfaced in the course of the study, I
thought it would be helpful to give you some structured activities and exercises to consider. They're exercises and activities you
can carry out, particularly at the front end of a relationship, that
might keep you thinking rationally. If nothing else, the activities
and exercises will give you an opportunity to judge a potential
relationship in a more objective way.

In truth, there's no such thing as a sure-fire method to spot a
Romantic Liar, but some of the suggestions might help. Besides
that, the exercises and activities might help you spot a problem
partner, even if big-time lying isn't one of his problems. You may
choose to ignore the suggestions, thinking that what I'm suggesting takes a little of the romance out of a relationship. On the
other hand, with the potential for Romantic Deception being
what it is, it's hard to imagine that there's such a thing as too
much information about a potential partner. The choice is yours.

Exercises to Try at the Start
of a Relationship

Exercise #1

If you want to check out the information exchange that's
really going on in your relationship (particularly at the beginning), use the following guide to construct two lists. One should
be a list of *what your partner knows about you* (presumably
because you or others have told him), and the second should be

a list of *what you know about your potential partner* (particularly what he has told you about himself). Make the lists now. Don't cheat by waiting until you've spent more time with him—if you cheat, you're only cheating yourself. Treat the lists as though it were a series of questions. Answer all the questions you can, but put a question mark down if you don't have the answer. At a minimum, make certain you include each of the following. Add anything else that comes to mind.

- Name (first, middle, last)
- Current place of residence
- Previous places of residence
- Marital history
- Occupational history
- Educational background
- Military service background
- Religion
- Age/date of birth
- Family composition
- Friends, hobbies, etc.

Once you've made your lists, take a few minutes to look over what you've written. If the lists are terribly out of balance in his favor—in other words, if he knows far more about you than you know about him—it's time to seriously consider the possibility that you're involved in a deceptive relationship.

Exercise #2

Assuming you're getting involved in a new relationship, make a list (mentally or on paper) of how many times your new partner is calling you. Make a note of *where* you are *when* he calls (for example, at home or at work); *how often* he calls; and *what* the two of you talk about. Also make a similar list that tracks your activities—the *when*, *where*, and *what* of your time together.

If there's an abundance of truly meaningless telephone calls and they typically include your partner wanting to know the details of your schedule, a red flag should go up immediately. The same thing goes for a string of activities that always has the two of you alone and out of the company of anyone else.

Exercise #3

Reread the list of typical narrowing tactics listed in Section III. Mentally add others to the list if you've experienced them in other relationships. Write down each tactic in one column. Use a second column to complete an honest inventory on how many times you've seen each tactic surface in your present relationship. Use a third column to reconstruct how you felt when you witnessed the behavior and how you responded. It's this third column that's so important. Try to honestly write down your thoughts. *Did the behavior strike you as odd or inappropriate—how did you feel when it happened? Did it seem normal or OK?*

Be sure to note any times you deliberately started altering your behavior as a result of a narrowing tactic being used on you. Once you've done your work, take a few minutes to reread everything you've written. After you've done that, ask yourself one simple question: *Would I be willing to show this to a good friend?* Above all else, be honest in your answer. If you wouldn't want to show the list to your friends because you know they'd likely tell you to dump the guy, take that as a warning. Remember—you don't actually have to show your work to someone else; all you have to do is ask yourself how you'd feel if you did that. If you'd be embarrassed or uncomfortable, you're involved with the wrong person!

Exercise #4

Find a reason to alter your schedule radically and be *out of pocket* for a while. If your new partner normally calls you around 2:00 in the afternoon, just leave your house or take the afternoon off from work to do some shopping, run errands, visit a museum, or anything else you'd like to do. See what happens. See if he voices a concern about where you were. Carefully examine what he has to say and how he says it. Romantic Liars don't like their targets freely roaming around town. A major reaction on your partner's part is a clue to danger ahead.

Exercise #5

As a variation of that last exercise, plan a get-together with some of your female friends, and tell your new partner about it in advance. Tell him you're having a *girls' night out to dinner* sort of gathering. See how he reacts. Look for any reaction that signals his intolerance for your independence. To a Romantic Liar, your being in the company of good friends spells potential disaster. An informal dinner with friends amounts to a structured reality check as far as he's concerned—it gives you the chance to tell all your friends about him and his behaviors. Anyone at the table might start spewing forth *contradictory knowledge* about him—some kernel of truth that sheds light on the deception. That's why it can drive a Romantic Liar straight up the wall when you spend time with your friends. Remember—you're just starting a relationship with this guy. It's still your life—or it should be. If he doesn't see it that way, you're headed for trouble.

Resources for Early Detection

If there's a single, most disturbing aspect to Romantic Deception, it is this: So many cases of Romantic Deception I heard about could have been nipped in the bud so easily. In case after case a Romantic Liar could have been stopped in his tracks well before he had a chance to really begin weaving his web of deceit. All too often only two things stood in the way of early detection: a target's unwillingness to really check out a potential partner, and her lack of knowledge of how to go about it. This next bit of material is designed to take care of at least one of those missing ingredients. The material will give you some tools you can use to check out a potential partner, but the motivation and desire to do so is obviously up to you.

If you're short on the motivation, I would only remind you of what I mentioned earlier: In interview after interview, the women told me that they intended to be deliberately cautious in the future. Some stopped short of saying they would launch a full-scale background investigation, but even those women generally said they'd only date men they knew a lot about.

Far more, however, were certain they'd do some serious background checking in the future. What's more, they were pretty unshakable in their position. That was the way it was going to be. If a man came along who couldn't handle the thought of being checked out, that would be his problem. As one woman put it, *a man ought to be pleased that a woman would check him out—it should tell him that she doesn't just get involved with every guy that comes along.*

Assuming you're someone who wants to be more informed about the men you date, let me suggest you spend a little time with the material you're about to read. Even if it's material you don't need for reference right now, let it find a spot in your brain—somewhere you can reach for it when you think you need it in the future.

Public Records and Other Forms of Information

Before I introduce you to the world of public records, a sincere expression of gratitude is in order. A significant amount of the material you are about to read was made available through the generosity of Mr. Mike Sankey and his organization, BRB Publications. Much of the material was rewritten, with permission of Mr. Sankey, for use in this book.

Mr. Sankey, President of BRB Publications, is widely acknowledged as one of the nation's leading experts on public records, and his organization is regarded as a premier source on the use and availability of public records. The material and insights supplied by Mr. Sankey were invaluable to my effort.

If you're like most people, the expression *public records* can call forth all sorts of images—mysterious files located in out-of-the-way offices, out of the reach of most people and full of a lot of information that may be difficult to understand. To a lot of people, public records are of interest to only a select number of people— private investigators, law enforcement personnel, journalists, or attorneys who are tracking assets. As you'll soon see, however, public records are anything but mysterious, are hardly inaccessible, and, most important, are very likely to be of interest to you.

Let's start with a simple definition to give you an idea of what public records are all about and why you should have no hesitation in making use of them. Public records are records that are maintained by any number of government agencies—at the federal, county, and municipal levels of government (counties and cities, for example). As a rule, they constitute a record of some event—a marriage, a divorce, the birth of a child, the sale of a piece of property, and so on. Public records are *open* in the sense that they are generally available to you for your use without restrictions.

Strictly speaking, public records are records about incidents or actions filed with a government agency. The very purpose behind the record is to make it public. In other words, a public record serves to notify others (*the public*) about some incident or action. For example, when you purchase a home, the deed to your home is recorded with the county government and anyone is free to review a copy of the deed.

Even though what is meant by the term *public record* enjoys fairly widespread agreement, what records fall into the category of public records varies greatly. For your purposes, always remember that every state and county agency has its own legal view of the matter—what constitutes a public record varies from state to state and county to county. For example, in one state birth records or vehicle ownership records may be 100 percent open and accessible, but access to those same records may be severely restricted in another state.

Whenever you go looking for a public record, you're doing something that you or any citizen has a right to do. Public records exist for the benefit of the society. Public records are reviewed by all sorts of people every day for any number of purposes, and you, too, can review them. Remember—they are *public*.

Of course, not every bit of information held by government agencies is considered public, and the line that differentiates between public and nonpublic records is constantly changing. When it comes to trying to find out background information on someone, you will eventually discover that there's a lot of information out there, but not all of it falls into the public record category.

Apart from public records per se, there is another category of data known as *public information*. This is information that people have freely furnished, and it is also available to the public. Your telephone number listing in a local phone directory is a good example of public information. It is not a record of a specific event and the law does not require that it be recorded. On the other hand, it is public if you choose to have your telephone number listed in the telephone book or with directory assistance.

Personal information, on the other hand, includes any information about a person or business that might be considered private and confidential in nature. Your Social Security Number, for example, is personal information. As a rule, personal information remains relatively private and its access by others is generally limited.

It's a good idea to remember, however, that a significant amount of personal information will find its way into public records or public information. This is an important point to remember if your aim is to gather information on a potential partner. It's not unusual to review a public record document (for example, a copy of a mortgage document that has been filed at the county courthouse) and discover that it includes some personal information (such as a person's Social Security Number).

Although we generally think of public records as being housed in government agencies, there are any number of private individuals and companies that locate and sell all sorts of information. As a rule, you usually have a large menu of choices when it comes to how you want to go about reviewing public records. You'll find a discussion of some of those resources in a latter part of this section.

Depending on where you live, you may want to visit the primary source—the agency that actually maintains the public record files. For example, real-estate transactions and voter registration records are generally available at the county courthouse (or the county recorder's office). If you live in or nearby the county seat (the town that is the location of the county government), you may want to pay a personal visit to do your own on-site searching. Many county courthouse operations are extremely sophisticated, yet accessible. It is common to find computerized access to any number of county records. If you're looking for a birth record, you may have to go to a state/county office responsible for the collection of vital statistics (i.e., birth and death certificates). Again, what records are public and where they are located is subject to widespread variation from state to state. But once you determine where certain information is housed, you'll probably be surprised at just how accessible the records are and how helpful some of the records clerks can be. Public agency employees answer hundreds of questions a day. Answering questions is part of their job. Most will be more than happy to assist you.

Even if you have no reason to really do so, I recommend that you (and every other citizen, for that matter) take an hour or so to visit a county courthouse or records facility just to learn about all the information that is there and available. You never know when you might need it. If you visit the courthouse or a records facility in a large county (i.e., one that is heavily populated), you may discover that different types of records are kept in different locations, but usually all the buildings are close to one another. In the more rural areas and the counties with smaller populations, a single, centralized location of records is more the norm.

There are two reasons why a county courthouse is a good place to start anytime you're looking for public information of any sort. First, a lot of the information you're looking for may actually be housed at the county courthouse. Second, if the information is to be found somewhere else, the records clerks can probably steer you to the right source. If they cannot, they can probably steer you in the direction of someone who can get you on the right trail to the information you're after.

If you're actually searching for some specific information and it isn't convenient for you to pay a personal visit to an agency, you can usually make contact or submit your request via mail, fax, or telephone. Because so many public record databases are now stored on computers, agency personnel can usually locate records with relative ease. Therefore, some agencies can very easily answer your questions over the phone. However, you should be aware that the trend is toward fewer and fewer agencies providing information over the phone.

Although numerous agencies still accept phone requests for information, most agencies prefer mail or fax requests if you cannot request the information in person. Generally you can call the agency to see if it actually has the record you're looking for and to see what the fee will be. Since public records are records of incidents or transactions and it costs money to record these events, governmental agencies routinely charge copy fees and search fees. These fees can range from a few cents per page to copy a document to $15 or $20 for a search if agency personnel are required to locate the records. In some cases, higher fees are charged for *expedited services*.

Once you decide that there are some things about your partner that you want to check out, you'll probably determine that the county courthouse is the best place to start. As I mentioned earlier, if the information you're looking for isn't kept at the courthouse, some of the courthouse personnel can probably tell you where to find what you're looking for. That's all well and good, *provided* you know which county courthouse to go to or to contact. It all boils down to geography.

A Little Lesson in Geography

Let's say your partner told you he got a divorce two years ago, and he told you he *was living in Dallas* at the time he got the divorce. Unfortunately, you may not know exactly what your partner means when he says he was *living in Dallas*. For some people, the expression *living in Dallas* means they were living in the *Dallas area*. No matter how you look at it, the *Dallas area* is very large. For example, the City of Dallas actually extends into several counties, and Dallas County is only one of them. There are also numerous independent cities (separate city governments) located inside the city limits of the City of Dallas. Someone might live in a suburban city (located outside the city limits of the City of Dallas) and in some county other than Dallas County. Still that person might say he lives in Dallas.

How people refer to where they live is probably largely a function of local custom. Just because some people aren't highly specific when they make reference to where they live or lived doesn't mean they're up to something sinister or they're trying to hide something about their background. In most cases it's probably nothing more than a matter of custom and common usage.

What all this means when you want to check out public records—particularly those that are apt to be at the county courthouse—is that you have to know what county courthouse you want to deal with. To thoroughly check out the situation you may have to contact two or more of the county courthouses. Not every city is as large as Dallas, to be sure, but many cities extend into several counties. Therefore, my advice is simple: Always start your research by knowing where you're going with your research. If you are not certain about the geographic structure of an area, get a map and check it out. University and local libraries usually have a variety of map resources (either collections of individual maps or atlases). Bookstores are also an excellent source, particularly when you want the most current references. Some large

cities have retail stores that specialize in all sorts of geographi-
cally-oriented products—from maps to globes. Look in the
Yellow Pages directory under a listing for *maps* to see if there's
one in your area.

Once you've identified the county or counties where the
information is likely to be located, it's a good idea to make a
telephone call to get some basic information—such things as the
exact location of the building, where the records you're looking
for are stored, hours of operation, etc. As I mentioned before,
don't hesitate to ask the personnel to help you. I think you'll be
pleasantly surprised.

In some cases, of course, the information you're looking for
may have nothing to do with data collected by county or state
agencies. You may be in search of information about someone's
military history, for example, or you might be interested in verifying an educational background. To get an idea of just how
much information is available, where it's usually located, and
what you can learn from the information, take a look at the
material that follows.

Real-Estate Records

Among all the public records that exist, real-estate (property)
records are among the most accessible. Because records of real-estate
transactions are used in so many different situations by so many
people, they are searched and researched all day long. The fact that
you might want to take a look at the records is nothing new.

You can find property records at both the city and county
level. There will always be some property records at the county
level, but since many cities also derive revenue from property
taxes, property records can also exist at the city level. As a rule,
you can usually search for properties by name, street address, or
legal description (i.e., lot, block, and subdivision). If, for example, a potential partner invites you over to his home for dinner,
but your intuition tells you he really doesn't own the house, it is
a very simple matter to check it out. All you have to do is check

with the relevant taxing authorities (city or county) or registrar of deeds.

In many areas, all you have to do is place a telephone call to the tax assessor's office and ask who is listed as the owner of a property at a certain address. Call the local courthouse and ask for the numbers of the assessor's office and the registrar of deeds' office. When you're searching for information about a deed or other recorded information, you may discover that it is located in the county clerk's office (as opposed to the recorder or registrar of deeds' office).

The assessor's office will have tax and appraisal information on all the properties in the county, but the more detailed information will be in the recorder or registrar of deeds' office (copies of deeds, mortgages, liens, etc.). If you're unsure as to whether or not there is a city or municipal property taxing authority, ask while you're placing that same call. Most taxing authorities can easily give you the phone number of other taxing authorities in the area.

Once you've reached the assessor's office, the simplest way to phrase your inquiry is to tell the records clerk that you'd like to *check the ownership* on a certain piece of property. It's also a good idea to ask if you could have the name and mailing address of the person to whom the tax statements are sent. You never know what that question might turn up in the way of information. You should be aware that not every office is willing to conduct a search by name only. On the other hand, it never hurts to ask.

If you actually pay a visit to the courthouse, you can expand or extend your search with some potentially interesting outcomes. At the recorder or registrar of deeds' offices, you may learn that the information on a deed may or may not match up with what you were told over the telephone. For example, the taxing office should be able to report exactly how the property is listed on the deed, but mistakes do happen. The deed is the most official record of ownership. Who knows? You may find that your potential partner owns the property in question—and he owns it with his wife. More than one woman has checked the ownership records on a potential partner and discovered that very fact.

With so many governmental units putting their records into a computerized database, it's usually very easy to search the records database to determine all the properties owned by a given individual. You can also search the files for records of any tax or contractors liens that have been levied on the properties. By the same token, you can get copies of any mortgages on the properties, even if they've been paid off, and you might be surprised at what the mortgage document reveals (for example, a person's driver's license or Social Security Number may be entered on the document).

The task of tracing the ownership of a certain piece of property is also something that is usually fairly easy to do. Let's say that during that dinner at your potential partner's house he tells you he's actually sold the house and will be moving in a month or so. That's fine. He may be telling you the truth. If so, the sale of the property will eventually work its way into the public records—something else you can check if you want to. But if it's now six months down the road, the sale hasn't been recorded yet, and your potential partner is making noises about moving in with you, it's time for a reality check.

Again, let me emphasize a point I made earlier. Don't hesitate to ask the records agency personnel for assistance. The people who work for the various records agencies are generally very knowledgeable. If they can't give you an answer, they can generally steer you to someone who can. Many agencies have information desks located in lobby areas, and the people who work there are equally capable and able when it comes to pointing you in the right direction. I would also remind you to never forget that informal geography lesson you were introduced to earlier. Once you've had a look at the records in one county or city, you might want to spend a little time with the records in surrounding areas, particularly if the focus of your research is in a larger metropolitan area.

Marriage and Divorce Records

Marriage and divorce records make up part of what is generally referred to as *vital records* (the other parts are the birth and death records). Although marriage and divorce records can be very important sources of information when it comes to whether or not your potential partner is telling the truth, the research isn't quite as straightforward as it is in the case of property records. The reason is obvious, when you think about it. Property records are tied to a specific piece of property, and that means they are tied to a specific place, often the same place where you are living. Marriage and divorce records, however, are tied to events that could have occurred at any number of places.

Let's say, for example, that you've met someone who claims he got a divorce three years ago. So how do you know he's telling you the truth? You can tell him you'll need to see a copy of the divorce decree (remember—you'll want to see a file-stamped copy that gives the case number and date), or you could do your own investigation. If you decide to do your own verification, the problem is you have to know where the divorce was granted (in other words, in what county).

If the guy in question has told you he was living in Kansas City, for example, you'll have to tackle the problem of geography I mentioned earlier. Unfortunately, in a place like Kansas City, the problem is magnified. You'll have to determine if you want to research the *Kansas* part of Kansas City or the *Missouri* part of Kansas City. Beyond that, there's still the problem of exactly which county to research. Again, like so many other large cities, the area referred to as the *Kansas City area* actually extends into several counties.

Once you think you've got a pretty good idea of where the divorce took place (i.e., what county), you can call the courthouse and make a telephone inquiry. You may want to start with a general inquiry to the *information line* at the courthouse. Once you're connected to the appropriate office, politely ask if it is possible to get information concerning a divorce record by phone. Again, that is the type of question records clerks are used to answering hundreds of times every day. Don't hesitate to ask.

You'll generally need to have the name or names of the parties involved and an approximate date—for example, a range of several years. If you learn that a record exists, be certain to ask when the court action was filed and *when it was final*. A lot of divorce proceedings are initiated, but that doesn't mean the parties go through with them. A divorce is said to have been *finaled* when the divorce decree is actually granted. How much of the information connected with a divorce is available and open to public inspection will necessarily vary from jurisdiction to jurisdiction. It's always worth asking because you might be astonished what some of the records could yield in the way of information (such things as the grounds for the divorce, presence of children in the marriage, assets, etc.).

In a similar manner, you might not turn up a record of a divorce, but simply making a telephone call might yield some very unexpected information. One woman, for example, made a telephone call to inquire whether or not there were any divorces on file for the man she was dating, only to be told something that had never crossed her mind. The clerk on the other end of the phone said there weren't any divorces on file, but there was a *victim's protective order*. Since a victim's protective order is something taken against someone who has been threatening or violent, the information was very valuable to say the least. The clerk went on to tell the woman that she wasn't supposed to give out that information unless she was specifically asked that question. The woman who was making the call understood exactly what was being said, in an oh-so-subtle way, so she rephrased her question on the spot. With that, the clerk started spewing forth the date of the protective order along with the name of the person who had obtained it. It turned out that the man's previous girlfriend was the one who took out the protective order. No divorce records, but some mighty valuable information!

Birth and Death Records

Like marriage and divorce records, the public information on births and deaths is part of what is often referred to as *vital* records. As with so many other records, a good place to begin your inquiry is with a call to a general information line at the county courthouse. Birth records can be a valuable source of information if you're attempting to determine whether or not your partner has any children that he has failed to mention. Likewise, a review of death records might give you a clue to whether or not your partner is telling a personal tragedy lie if he says his parents are deceased. You will likely discover that the birth and death records are located at the county health department or a state government office. The listing that follows provides you with some addresses and phone numbers that will link you to sources that can give you specific details on the location of vital records in each state.

Also see the following Web site: http://www.cdc.gov/nch-swww. Once you're there, click on the "how to" button to learn where to write for records.

Alabama
Center for Health Statistics
State Department of Public Health
PO Box 5625
Montgomery, AL 36103-5625
Telephone: (334) 206-5418

Alaska
Department of Health and Social
  Services
Bureau of Vital Statistics
PO Box 110675
Juneau, AK 99811-0675
Telephone: (907) 465-3391

Arizona
Vital Records Section
Arizona Department of Health
  Services
PO Box 3887
Phoenix, AZ 85030
Telephone: (602) 255-3260

Arkansas
Division of Vital Records
Arkansas Department of Health
4815 West Markham Street
Little Rock, AR 72205
Telephone: (501) 661-2336

California
Office of Vital Records
Department of Health Services
PO Box 730241
Sacramento, CA 94244-0241
Telephone: (916) 445-2684

Colorado
Vital Records Section
Colorado Department of Public
  Health and Environment
4300 Cherry Creek Drive South
HSVRD-VS_A1
Denver, CO 80246-1530
Telephone: (303) 756-4464

Connecticut
Vital Records
Department of Public Health
150 Washington St.
Hartford, CT 06106
Telephone: (203) 566-2334

Delaware
Office of Vital Statistics
Division of Public Health
PO Box 637
Dover, DE 19903
Telephone: (302) 739-4721

District of Columbia
Vital Records Branch
800 9th Street, SW
1st Floor
Washington, DC 20024
Telephone: (202) 645-5962

Florida
Department of Health and
  Rehabilitative Services
Office of Vital Statistics
PO Box 210
1217 Pearl Street
Jacksonville, FL 32231
Telephone: (904) 359-6900

Georgia
Georgia Department of Human
  Resources
Vital Records Service
Room 217-H
47 Trinity Avenue, SW
Atlanta, GA 30334
Telephone: (404) 656-4900

Hawaii
State Department of Health
Office of Health Status
  Monitoring
Vital Records Section
PO Box 3378
Honolulu, HI 96801-9984
Telephone: (808) 586-4533

Idaho
Vital Statistics Unit
Center for Vital Statistics and
  Health Policy
450 West State Street, 1st Floor
PO Box 83720
Boise, ID 83720-0036
Telephone: (208) 334-5988

Illinois
Division of Vital Records
Illinois Department of Public
  Health
605 West Jefferson Street
Springfield, IL 62702-5097
Telephone: (217) 782-6553

Indiana
Vital Records Section
State Department of Health
2 North Meridian Street
Indianapolis, IN 46204
Telephone: (317) 233-2700

Iowa
Iowa Department of Public Health
Vital Records Section
Lucas Office Building
321 East 12th Street
Des Moines, IA 50319-0075
Telephone: (515) 281-4944

Kansas
Office of Vital Statistics
Kansas State Department of
  Health and Environment
Landon State Office Building
900 SW Jackson Street, Rm. 151
Topeka, KS 66612-2221
Telephone: (785) 296-1400

Kentucky
Office of Vital Statistics
Department of Health Services
275 East Main Street
Frankfort, KY 40621
Telephone: (502) 564-4212

Louisiana
Vital Records Registry
Office of Public Health
325 Loyola Avenue
New Orleans, LA 70112
Telephone: (504) 568-5152

Maine
Office of Vital Statistics
Maine Department of Human
  Services
State House Station 11
Augusta, ME 04333-0011
Telephone: (207) 287-3184

Maryland
Division of Vital Records
Department of Health and Mental
  Hygiene
6550 Reisterstown Road
PO Box 68760
Baltimore, MD 21215-0020
Telephone: (410) 764-3038

Massachusetts
Registry of Vital Records and
  Statistics
470 Atlantic Avenue, 2nd Floor
Boston, MA 02210-2224
Telephone: (617) 753-8600

Michigan
Vital Records
3423 North Martin Luther King
  Blvd.
PO Box 30195
Lansing, MI 48909
Telephone: (517) 335-8656

Minnesota
Minnesota Department of Health
Section of Vital Statistics
717 Delaware Street, SE
PO Box 9441
Minneapolis, MN 55440
Telephone: (612) 676-5120

Mississippi
Vital Records
State Department of Health
2423 North State Street
Jackson, MS 39216
Telephone: (601) 576-7981

Missouri
Missouri Department of Health
  Bureau of Vital Records
930 Wildwood
PO Box 570
Jefferson City, MO 65102-0570
Telephone: (573) 751-6400

Montana
MT Department of Public Health
  and Human Services
Vital Statistics Bureau
PO Box 4210
Helena, MT 59604
Telephone: (406) 444-4228

Nebraska
Bureau of Vital Statistics
Department of Health and
  Human Services
301 Centennial Mall South
PO Box 95065
Lincoln, NE 68509-5065
Telephone: (402) 471-2871

Nevada
Division of Health-Vital Statistics
Capitol Complex
505 East King Street #102
Carson City, NV 89710
Telephone: (775) 687-4480

New Hampshire
Bureau of Vital Records
Health and Welfare Building
6 Hazen Drive
Concord, NH 03301
Telephone: (603) 271-4654

New Jersey
New Jersey State Department of
  Health and Senior Services
Bureau of Vital Statistics
PO Box 370
Trenton, NJ 08625
Telephone: (609) 292-4087

New Mexico
Vital Statistics
New Mexico Health Services
  Division
PO Box 26110
Santa Fe, NM 87502
Telephone: (505) 827-2338

**New York (Except New York
  City)**
Certification Unit
Vital Records Section
PO Box 2602
Albany, NY 12220-2602
Telephone: (518) 474-3075

New York City
Office of Vital Records
New York City Department of Health
125 Worth Street, Box 4
New York, NY 10013
Telephone: (212) 788-4520

North Carolina
NC Vital Records
PO Box 29537
Raleigh, NC 27626-0537
Telephone: (919) 733-3526

North Dakota
Division of Vital Records
State Capitol
600 East Boulevard Avenue
Bismarck, ND 58505-0200
Telephone: (701) 328-2360

Ohio
Bureau of Vital Statistics
Ohio Department of Health
PO Box 15098
Columbus, OH 43215-0098
Telephone: (614) 466-2531

Oklahoma
Vital Records Section
State Department of Health
1000 Northeast 10th Street
PO Box 53551
Oklahoma City, OK 73152
Telephone: (405) 271-4040

Oregon
Oregon Health Division
Vital Statistics Section
PO Box 14050
Portland, OR 97293-0050
Telephone: (503) 731-4095

Pennsylvania
Division of Vital Records State
   Department of Health
Central Building
101 South Mercer Street
PO Box 1528
New Castle, PA 16103
Telephone: (724) 656-3100

Rhode Island
Division of Vital Records
Rhode Island Department of
   Health
3 Capitol Hill, Rm. 101
Providence, RI 02908-5097
Telephone: (401) 222-2811

South Carolina
Office of Public Health Statistics
   and Information Systems
South Carolina Department of
   Health and Environmental
   Control
2600 Bull Street
Columbia, SC 29201
Telephone: (803) 734-4830

South Dakota
Vital Records
State Department of Health
600 East Capitol Avenue
Pierre, SD 57501-2536
Telephone: (605) 773-3355

Tennessee
Tennessee Vital Records
Department of Health Central
   Services Building
421 5th Avenue, North
Nashville, TN 37247-0450
Telephone: (615) 741-1763

Texas
Bureau of Vital Statistics
Texas Department of Health
PO Box 12040
Austin, TX 78711-2040
Telephone: (512) 458-7111

Utah
Bureau of Vital Records
Utah Department of Health
288 North 1460 West
PO Box 141012
Salt Lake City, UT 84114-1012
Telephone: (801) 538-6105

Vermont
Vermont Department of Health
Vital Records Section
PO Box 70
108 Cherry Street
Burlington, VT 05402
Telephone: (802) 863-7275

Virginia
Office of Vital Records and Health
   Statistics
State Health Department
PO Box 1000
Richmond, VA 23218-1000
Telephone: (804) 225-5000

Washington
Department of Health
Center for Health Statistics
PO Box 9709
Olympia, WA 98507-9709
Telephone: (360) 236-4300

West Virginia
Vital Registration Office
Division of Health State
Capitol Complex Bldg. 3
Charleston, WV 25305
Telephone: (304) 558-2931

Wisconsin
Vital Records
1 West Wilson Street
PO Box 309
Madison, WI 53701
Telephone: (608) 266-1371

Wyoming
Vital Records Services
Hathaway Building
Cheyenne, WY 82002
Telephone: (307) 777-7591

Social Security Numbers

If you happen to know your partner's Social Security Number, you're in a better position to find out more about him. Not only can the Social Security Number give you access to information that you might not otherwise be able to obtain, but the Social Security Number by itself can tell you something about your partner's background.

Since the numbers used in the assignment of Social Security Numbers are coded by the state in which the number was issued, knowledge of your partner's social security number could prove to be revealing. For example, let's say that your partner has never said a word about having lived in North Carolina. Since he's never even mentioned that state, you probably wouldn't think too much about it. You wouldn't have any reason to, at least not in the context of your partner and his life history. But what if your partner's Social Security Number reveals that he was living in North Carolina at the time the card was issued? Is that something that would get your attention? The list that follows will allow you to determine where an individual was living at the time the card was issued (if it was issued in 1972 or later) or the location of the Social Security office that issued the card (before 1972).

The first three digits of a person's Social Security Number actually constitute what is known as an area number. Before 1972, the first three numbers in a person's Social Security Number indicated which social security field office issued the card. Since 1972, the first three digits indicate the place of residence of the individual requesting the card. Most of the three-digit codes refer back to specific states. The exceptions are certain three-digit numbers that were reserved for railroad employees before 1964 (regardless of where they were residing at the time they requested a card), and numbers for areas outside the fifty states, such as the Pacific Islands (Guam, American Samoa, etc.), Puerto Rico, and the Virgin Islands.

The following list provides the three-digit ranges of numbers, along with the corresponding state or area. Since new numbers are being placed into service as the demand for additional Social

Security Numbers continues to increase, you should always contact the Social Security Administration for the most up-to-date information.

001–003 NH	400–407 KY	530 NV
004–007 ME	408–415 TN	531–539 WA
008–009 VT	416–424 AL	540–544 OR
010–034 MA	425–428 MS	545–573 CA
035–039 RI	429–432 AR	574 AK
040–049 CT	433–439 LA	575–576 HI
050–134 NY	440–448 OK	577–579 DC
135–158 NJ	449–467 TX	580–584 Puerto Rico, Virgin Islands
159–211 PA	468–477 MN	585 NM
212–220 MD	478–485 IA	586 Pacific Islands
221–222 DE	486–500 MO	587–588 MS
223–231 VA	501–502 ND	589–595 FL
232–236 WV	503–504 SD	596–599 Puerto Rico
232; 237–246 NC	505–508 NE	600–601 AZ
247–251 SC	509–515 KS	602–626 CA
252–260 GA	516–517 MT	627–645 TX
261–267 FL	518–519 ID	646–647 UT
268–302 OH	520 WY	648–649 NM
303–317 IN	521–524 CO	
318–361 IL	525 NM	
362–386 MI	526–527 AZ	
387–399 WI	528–529 UT	

Up-to-date information concerning Social Security Number assignment by state can be found by contacting the following Web site: http://www.itsc.state.md.us/prog_info/SSA/ssnalloc.html.

Voter Registration Records

Voter registration records can be found at either the state or county levels of government. Like so many other types of public records, availability and access varies greatly from state to state. An easy way to find out what the policy is in a particular state is to call a general information line at the county courthouse and request the telephone number of the *local election board* or the *registrar of voters* (the name of the office varies from county to county). Regardless of the specific name, what you're looking for is the body that supervises elections. Personnel from the local election board can then answer your questions about the availability of voter registration information and what rules govern accessibility. Once again there is great variation from state to state as to what information is released, but you can find some valuable information in the files, assuming you gain access. For example, it is common for Social Security Numbers to appear on a person's voter registration form. In some areas access to that part of the record is blocked, but that isn't the case in all states.

If you are lucky enough to be searching in a county that has its files computerized (and that's the case in a significant number of counties), you may find some very valuable information even if the Social Security Number is blocked. For example, with a computerized search system, you might type in the last name of the individual you're checking out and get a listing of the names of all registered voters with the same last name. If the list also has addresses, you might find other individuals living at the same address as the person you're researching—for example, a wife or children who are old enough to register.

Because voter registration data can be such a valuable source of information, you are well advised to investigate exactly what information is available for the area where you are focusing your research interest. If you can get access to individual records, you might find more than you ever thought you would. Even if the Social Security Number is blocked, you might find that there's no restriction on making available the person's date of birth.

Educational Records

As I mentioned earlier, lies about educational background are actually quite common. Among all the various status variables that men lie about, tall tales about educational achievements appear to top the list. Fortunately, it's usually fairly easy to check up on someone's claim about his educational background. As a rule, it is almost impossible to get a copy of a former student's *transcript* (a record of the student's academic performance), but it can be a relatively simply matter to determine if someone actually attended a certain college or university.

Since employers routinely want to verify a potential employee's educational credentials, colleges and universities have grown accustomed to providing relevant information along those lines. The information is usually housed in the *registrar's office*. Some schools might require that you have the Social Security Number of the person in question, but you might be able to get the information without it. Be prepared to provide an approximate range of years when you think the person in question may have been in attendance, along with full name and date of birth (if you have it).

Most schools will provide what is known as *matriculation information* (enrollment or attendance data) verification over the telephone, but some may require a written request. A simple phone call to the university (again, it's usually the registrar's office that you'll want to contact) will get you the information on what's necessary to request the record. My advice, though, is just to make the call as though you know what you're doing (as in, *Good morning—I'm calling to verify the enrollment record of a former student*). You might mention that you aren't calling to get a transcript—you just want to *verify attendance*.

As you might expect, there's usually a limit on how specific the information will be. For example, most universities will verify for you the dates of enrollment, academic major or course of study, date(s) of graduation, and degree(s) received (if any). Some will tell you if there was any official participation in varsity athletics.

Don't expect to get someone's grade point average, however. There's simply a limit on what the schools can or are willing to reveal. As a rule, your primary goal will probably be to establish that someone actually attended a certain school (and graduated, if that's the claim).

There's another information source that can be valuable if the man you're dating claims to hold a Ph.D. It's a reference work known as *Dissertation Abstracts*. Everyone who *earns* a Ph.D. (as opposed to an honorary doctorate) will have written a dissertation, and there is a record of the dissertation in *Dissertation Abstracts*. A copy of this publication can usually be found in the library of most universities. Some libraries access the publication via computer technology. Once you get access to *Dissertation Abstracts*, it's a fairly easy matter to confirm whether or not the claim of holding the Ph.D. degree is legitimate. If the claim is legitimate, the information should be there—the person's name, the university he attended, and when he was awarded the degree—including a brief abstract of what's included in the dissertation.

If you want to make use of the publication, call the nearest university library and ask to speak to the *reference librarian*. Since *Dissertation Abstracts* is a rather specialized publication, it's a good idea to confirm that you're actually talking to the reference librarian (as opposed to a student worker). That's not to take anything away from student workers; it's just that you may have several questions that you'll want to ask the librarian (where the publication is kept, whether or not it is accessed via computer, etc.). As I said, *Dissertation Abstracts* is a specialized publication—one that may be a little beyond the knowledge level of many student workers.

Military Records

Like higher education, service in the military is something that can be verified fairly easily. The Freedom of Information Act makes it possible for you to obtain a significant amount of information about your partner's service in the military. By the same token, if he claims he's been in the military, but there's no record of service, you've got a problem on your hands. Particularly in those cases where a suitor has spun a few tales about significantly heroic service to his country, a request for information may be very telling. Your partner may have actually served his country, but his purported list of awards and decorations might not match up with reality. To obtain information concerning whether someone is *currently* in the military, write to the following:

Army
Commander
U.S. Army Enlisted Records and Evaluation Center
Attn: Locator
Fort Benjamin
Harrison, IN 46249-5301

Navy
Chief of Naval Personnel
Bureau of Naval Personnel
(PERS-312D)
2 Navy Annex
Washington, DC 20370-5312

Air Force
HQ AFMPC/RMIQL
550 C Street, West, Suite 50
Randolph AFB, TX 78150-4752

Marine Corps
Commandant of the Marine Corps
Headquarters, USMC
Code MMSB-10
Quantico, VA 22134-5030

Coast Guard
Commandant of the Coast Guard
2100 Second Street, Southwest
Washington, DC 20593-0201

Additional information about identifying or locating *current* military personnel is available at the following Web site: http://www. defenselink.mil.faq/pis/PC04MLTR.html.

Under the Freedom of Information Act you are entitled to information on a *prior* service individual's full name, rank, salary, decorations/awards, previous duty assignments, and attendance at military schools. All you have to do is write to the National Personnel Records Center (NPRC) at the following location:

National Personnel Records Center
9700 Page Blvd.
St. Louis, MO 63132

The NPRC facility houses more than 50 million service records. In 1973, a fire destroyed approximately 13 million records (including a substantial number of records on army personnel discharged between 1912 and 1959). When requesting information from the NPRC, you will need to send the request as a letter or on a Form 180. You can request a copy of Form 180 by writing the NPRC facility or going to the NPRC Web site at the following Internet address: http://www.nara.gov/regional/mpr.html. You can download a copy of Form 180 from this site. You should note that the release portion of the form (which calls for a release signature from the veteran in question) only applies when requesting health information.

Professional or Occupational Associations

If someone claims to have a certain occupation and the claim is legitimate, there's a good chance that person's name will appear in some type of professional or occupational association directory. If the name doesn't appear, it may mean only that he isn't a member. On the other hand, it could raise a red flag in your mind. Local associations (metropolitan or county) of physicians, attorneys, and real-estate brokers or agents are examples of organizations that are commonplace. If someone tells you he's an attorney, it would be a simple matter to call the local *bar association* to see if he's a member.

Telephone/Address Records

Telephone and address listings actually fall into a category that information professionals refer to as *personal records*. They are records or bits of information about individuals, but they aren't necessarily public in the sense that you're guaranteed access to them. Many people, for example, choose not to have their names and/or addresses published in local telephone directories.

That is not to say, however, that many personal records don't find their way into public record databases. As I mentioned in an earlier example, a person's mailing address may show up on a property tax record. If that mailing address is the person's place of residence, it amounts to the same information that would appear in a telephone directory, had the person allowed the name and address to be published.

There are a lot of reasons why a person would request that his name and/or address not appear in the local telephone directory (*a nonpublished number*), so the fact that you can't find a listing for a potential partner may signal nothing in the way of deception. For that matter, it may not appear simply because he moved to town too recently for it to appear. Usually, a call to the local information operator will tell you whether that is the case.

Even though someone, for whatever reason, elects to have a nonpublished number, that doesn't mean you can't locate it. For example, it could appear in an earlier version of a telephone directory (say one that is two or three years old), and many public libraries keep copies of previous telephone directories, at least a few years back.

Many public libraries also have available reference books known as *reverse directories* (sometimes known as crisscross directories).

These directories allow you to identify telephone numbers associated with specific addresses and addresses that are associated with specific telephone numbers. If you have someone's home address, for example, you might be able to obtain the home telephone number through one of the reverse directories.

If you're looking into the background of someone who has an e-mail account, there's a chance you can find a relevant address and telephone number in one of the many e-mail directories available over the Internet. Most e-mail directories allow you to search for people by entering a minimal amount of information (for example, first and last name, along with city and/or state). Many of the directory services contain telephone and address information along with the e-mail listings. Reverse directories (including e-mail reverse directories) are also available through the Internet.

Using the Internet to Locate Records

By now it should be obvious: The recent revolution in computer technology has radically altered the picture. As much of the material you've just read demonstrates, a lot of the information is available through the Internet. With the advent of the Internet, the world of public records has become increasingly accessible, and the amount of available information is increasing on a daily basis. Instead of having to pay a personal visit to a state or local agency to search records, users of the Internet will find that some of the databases are available electronically.

Several state and local agencies have made significant portions of their public records available through the Internet, and there are other sites on the Internet that act as gateways to public records resources. Though direct or indirect Internet access to public records is still far from commonplace, the trend is growing. Every day there are new sites being added—some sites created and maintained by state and local agencies, other sites created and maintained by private information brokerages.

To find out if a particular state or local government agency has its own site and database access, use a search engine such as

Yahoo or Infoseek to determine what is available. For example, if you're interested in locating tax assessor information for County X, use the search engine of your choice to find sites associated with County X. If you find a specific listing for something along the lines of *County X: Offices and Resources*, it would be worth taking a look. You might find a sublisting for the tax assessor's office. Once you link to the tax assessor's office, you might find that the property tax records are accessible on-line and at no cost. The same thing may apply with respect to the tax assessor's office in a city government (assuming the city collects property tax).

By the same token, a search for state agencies (once you're in the *State of X* site) might turn up links to all or almost all the state agencies. If there is a link to the Secretary of State's office, you may be able to access information about corporations (officers, registered agents, etc.). Even if you can't have direct access to the database, the site may give you the information you need to submit a request by mail.

Similarly, surfing around a county or state site could yield specific information on how to get birth or death certificate information (such things as where the information is housed, what is necessary to gain access, costs, location addresses, phone numbers, etc.). As I said before, new sites are being added to the Internet every day. Many government agencies are working to make public records more available and on-line. As a result, you would probably be more and more amazed every day at what is available and within easy reach, assuming you have access to the Internet and just the most elementary knowledge of how to use it.

In addition to using the various state and local government sites (either through direct or indirect links), access to public records can also be gained through private sources—companies that offer on-line access to public records for a fee. These services often provide access to databases that would not normally be available on-line. Many states, for example, sell certain databases to the companies, and the companies, in turn, sell the information to individuals.

For example, in a particular state you might not be able to have direct on-line access to the state's motor vehicle registration database (to obtain license plate information), but you might be able to get to the database through an intermediary commercial service. The charge to get the license plate information could range from as little as $2 per plate to $5 or $10, depending on what intermediary service you go through and what state records are being accessed. By the same token, the voter registration records in a particular county might not be accessible on-line by private individuals, but you might be able to go through one of these third-party or intermediary data providers who has purchased the entire database.

As you might expect, the companies vary greatly in terms of what sort of information they can provide. The more full-service operations can provide information on everything from voter registration data to divorce records. Some of these companies are specialized by state or region. For example, one company may focus on public records data in one state while another company has its focus on an entirely different state. By the same token, some companies specialize in providing access to state or local government records in the western United States; others may have a mid-western focus.

As a rule, companies that provide information for a fee list the types of data they have, along with the costs (usually on a per search or per record basis), instructions on how to request the information, and estimated turnaround time on requests. Some companies only take requests; others make it possible for you to establish your own account, which in turn allows you to do your own searching of their files (the files they have actually purchased from the government agencies). With your own account you may be charged a per search or per record fee, or your account (with prepayment) may allow you to conduct a certain number of searches, up to a predetermined maximum.

Since many of the information brokers and companies in this general category owe their financial success to the Internet, that is where you will find many of them listed. A general search on one or more of the standard search engines using terms such as *public records* or *public data* should yield numerous listings for your consideration. Typical of what you might find would be the following:

> U.S.RecordSearch.com, at toll-free telephone 1-800-552-9279 or http://www.usrecordsearch.com/index.htm, offers research on matters such as addresses, assets, auto tags, court actions, death records, marriages and divorces, and real-estate records.
>
> The American Information Network, another public information data provider (located on the Internet at http://www.ameri. com/intro.htm), provides research services on consumer credit, educational history, bankruptcies, tax liens, and much more.

You can also contact knowX at knowX.com on the Internet. Like the other sites I've mentioned, knowX provides a full range of information services.

There are currently more than two hundred companies offering on-line access to proprietary databases of public record information. For an excellent listing of public record providers that includes on-line sources, you might want to consider a publication by the title of Public Records Online—The National Guide to Private and Government Sources of Public Records. This reference book can help you locate any number of companies that can assist you (for a fee) in your search of information. The book (published by Facts on Demand Press) is available through local bookstores or through BRB Publications (toll-free telephone 1-800-929-3811).

Other Internet Sites

A good example that will demonstrate the various types of links to public records is found in the following site: http://www.inil. com/users/dguss/wgator.htm—a project developed by an individual for the purpose of making public records available to large numbers of people. If you're an Internet user and you go to this Webgator site, you'll discover a lengthy list of links to any number of information sources. Here's a truncated list of what you'll find:

- Links to sites for bankruptcy and property records
- Numerous e-mail directories
- Links to various state agencies that house vital statistics information (birth, death, marriage, and divorce records)
- Links to Department of Motor Vehicles agencies in several states

Another site currently offering free access to a large number of databases is http://www.docusearch.com/free.html—when you discover how much information is available (and at no cost), you may be amazed.

Other Data Resources

If you want someone else to do the research for you, you may have to hire a licensed private investigator or other information brokers who offer more individual services. Many of the people offering services along these lines can be contacted via the Internet, as well as by phone, fax, or mail. Information professionals in this category can give you feedback on questions you might have about what certain types of information will tell you, and they can offer suggestions about what information might be worthwhile for your purposes.

Indeed, it is a statement of our times that some services along these lines are specifically marketed as a way to check out potential partners. Individuals or agencies providing these services are generally capable of providing background investigative services, often of the exact sort that would answer questions you might have about the truthfulness of someone's claims. You can enlist the services for a fee that is probably far less than what you might anticipate. In many cases, your interest may be for a level of information that stops well short of a complete investigation. For example, DateSmart, which maintains an Internet site at http://datesmart. com, specializes in background public records research, and specifically markets its services as geared toward checking out a potential partner. Among the services it offers are research on name verification, criminal history, motor vehicle information, civil filings (e.g., bankruptcies, tax liens, etc.), educational records, property ownership, marriage records, and divorce records. You can also contact Date Smart through a toll-free telephone number: 1-888-4CHECK (1-888-842-4325) or by e-mail at incase@gte.net.

If you know exactly what information or file you want, but it's in a courthouse located halfway across the country, there is an entire category of people known as information retrievers who can be of assistance. The retrievers are people who are generally very familiar with the location and content of records in their area. The number of people functioning as public record retrievers demonstrates the demand for services of this sort. There are more than 700 members of the Public Record Retrievers Network, and their services extend throughout the United States. More information about the use of retrievers can be found at www.publicrecordsource.com. For another excellent reference on what to look for when you're trying to locate a retriever and how to contact one, you might want to contact BRB Publications (1-800-929-3811) and request a copy of *The Sourcebook of Local Court and County Record Retrievers*.

Reference Works

If you're truly serious about wanting to protect yourself now or in the future, you may want to consult one or more of the numerous published sources that are available. The books are usually written by *information professionals*—people who have extensive backgrounds and experience in investigative activities—and they are targeted toward a wide market. Some of the books may be more appropriate reading for people who are in the information brokering business, but many are written for the general public and are available at local bookstores.

For an extensive listing of publications in this category, you might want to contact BRB Publications—the company I mentioned earlier. BRB Publications acts as something of a clearinghouse on publications related to public records and information brokering and carries an extensive list of publications. To request a catalogue—something I highly recommend you do—you can contact them through the number I referenced earlier or through their Web site at http://www.brbpub. com. You will find that it's very interesting.

The Decision Is Yours

Different people have very different opinions about whether or not it is appropriate to look into the background of a partner or potential partner. Some women, for example, would never even entertain the thought—either because they are naive to a fault or they have a genuine respect for the privacy of others. There are other women, however, who wouldn't think about getting seriously involved with someone without running a background check. Somewhere in the middle are women who are inclined to do a little sleuthing, but who fear how their partner or potential partner might react.

It's neither my job nor my inclination to tell any woman what she should do when it comes to the question of whether or not to look into someone's background. For many, the question revolves around values—values about privacy. For others, the idea is repugnant because it seems to violate the essence of romance or love or trust. All of those are big ideas, so I'm not about to debate them.

All I can do is emphasize what my research has told me, and that is the same message you've seen repeated throughout this book: Romantic Deception is something that happens to thousands of women every day. It is an experience that can be life-altering in many ways. It is a high-stakes game of the first order—one you're sure to lose if the game goes on too long.

A Romantic Liar doesn't introduce himself and then announce that he's looking forward to deceiving you, so you're only deceiving yourself if you think you can't fall victim. If he has his game down to an art, you'll be well into the relationship before you really have any serious suspicions that something is wrong. When everything finally comes to light, you'll probably be emotionally hooked to the point that the sense of betrayal will only be magnified.

There's a way to avoid a lot of that. It's called being wise and prudent and careful. It takes the form of your caring enough about yourself that you're willing to protect yourself. And looking into the background of a potential partner is essential if you really want to shield yourself from the possibility of undue harm.

As a practical matter, the sooner you check out a potential partner the better. An early investigation can be an early warning—often with the added benefit that you haven't reached the stage of being emotionally hooked. Without the emotional hook you can be more rational in interpreting the information in front of you, and any necessary exit from the relationship will be easier. Without the emotional hook you're also not as likely to have many fears about how your potential partner might react if he found out you were doing a little sleuthing.

When you make the decision to look into the background of a potential partner, you're making a statement to yourself and anybody else who has an interest in what you're doing. You're making a statement that you have a high regard for your own well-being. At a minimum, it is an act of high self-esteem. The choice is yours.

Index